ENCOUNTERS with AN ENLIGHTENED MAN

ENLIGHTENED MAN

The Early Years with Sydney Banks

BY LINDA QUIRING

CCB Publishing
British Columbia, Canada

Encounters with an Enlightened Man:
The Early Years with Sydney Banks

Copyright ©2017 by Linda Quiring
ISBN-13   978-1-77143-339-6
First Edition

Library and Archives Canada Cataloguing in Publication
Quiring, Linda, 1944-, author
Encounters with an enlightened man : the early years with Sydney Banks
/ by Linda Quiring. -- First edition.
Issued in print and electronic formats.
ISBN 978-1-77143-339-6 (softcover).--ISBN 978-1-77143-340-2 (pdf)
Additional cataloguing data available from Library and Archives Canada

Cover and interior photo credits: All images contained herein
are © Linda Quiring.

Articles herein that originally appeared in the *Gulf Islands Driftwood*
newspaper are reproduced with permission.

Extreme care has been taken by the author to ensure that all information
presented in this book is accurate and up to date at the time of publishing.
Neither the author nor the publisher can be held responsible for any errors
or omissions. Additionally, neither is any liability assumed for damages
resulting from the use of the information contained herein.

Publisher: CCB Publishing
               British Columbia, Canada
               www.ccbpublishing.com

Linda Quiring has remained a close family friend for over 40 years. I remember Linda's early visits to our quaint seaside home, perched attentively on my grandmother's weathered couch, the room filled with laughter and joy. Linda's inaugural book *Island of Knowledge* remains the earliest written account of the period immediately following my father Sydney Banks' powerful spiritual re-birth. It is an important historical work, for that reason alone. In this new book, Linda presents a deeply personal chronicle of those early years, in a way only she can. Linda continues to write with a unique style and refreshing lack of pretension.

Dave Banks
London, UK
October 20, 2017

DEDICATION

Constantly these days, my thoughts return again and again to Sydney Banks, for without his vision, sense of humour and compassion for those of us lost in the dream, these memories would never have come to life again.

Thank you, Syd.

ACKNOWLEDGMENTS

This book has been in my mind, thoughts and heart for almost a decade. When I began to reminisce about The Early Days; people, events, teachings and memories began to inspire me to do just that. I don't believe at that time I thought this project would ever come to fruition. Yet just as fate led me to Sydney Banks, it somehow made this book a reality and I need to thank those who somehow, together and apart, made that happen. Jim Beck, Jim and Judy Wallace, there in the very beginning were happy to contribute their stories, along with Sheri Hickman, and we all have remained friends through these four decades. I have always been supported in both my many adventures and misadventures by my family; Gary, Amber and Owen, and especially Bill, who continues to make lunch so that I can type. Dave Banks inspired me and our irregular chats made that past come alive in such a warm and loving way. Can't say enough about my publisher, Paul Rabinovitch who could not be easier to work with! Throughout this project and the two books that came before, the mind, heart and hand of Jack Pransky have been the glue that held it all together. Jack and I wrestled over events, memories, ups and downs, what to leave in, what to take out. Without him, The Early Days of Syd's work may well have vanished into the mists of time. I am grateful to you all!

ENCOUNTERS WITH AN ENLIGHTENED MAN

FOREWORD
by Jack Pransky

I have always been interested in history, beginning in elementary school on into the present—even the history of folk and rock music. In my previous field of prevention (of problem behaviors) I became a student of prevention history. My interest in Three Principles/Sydney Banks history is no exception; it prompted me to write the historical Three Principles book, *Paradigm Shift*, as well as *Modello*.

A gap in my historical knowledge nagged at me. What must it have been like in the very early days with Sydney Banks? How did it all get started? It must have been fascinating. So, I inquired; I asked questions. And when the opportunity presented itself through Linda Quiring I jumped at the chance.

I believe a historical record is important so we know from whence we came. Everything unfolded as it did for a reason and brought us to the present moment. Mistakes are made in history; if we are wise, we learn from them.

I am sure Syd came to have great reasons why he never talked about the very early days before psychologists George Pransky and Roger Mills came along, why as early as 1977 or 1978 he never pointed people in that direction, never talked about *Island of Knowledge* and almost seemed to disavow this early past. I would venture a strong guess that Syd believed if the world of professional psychology knew the early history of the group that originally had gathered around him it would have been detrimental to his message getting out to the world, and Syd wanted nothing more than for this incredible message to get out by whatever means necessary to be most helpful to humanity.

So, for those of us who desire to examine this early history, are we doing a disservice to Syd and the Three Principles "movement" by now revealing it? I think not. So much water has gone under the bridge since then. Three Principles understanding has taken on a life of its own and now cannot be stopped as it spreads throughout the world. In my view, it can no longer be detrimental to the message to now bring this history out into the light. To the contrary, I believe it can only be helpful. Syd had no choice but to start with those who first came to listen. To their credit, these first people did. A group formed around him. It served as a springboard for all that followed. After reading this history I came to believe Syd learned very much from this early experience, and the rest of us have benefitted enormously. We can learn from it, too.

As with *Paradigm Shift*, the various people involved in the early years will have their own different memories and views of what transpired back then and what they believe is important. They are welcome to write their own stories. History is as fluid as people's thoughts and memories. But Linda Quiring, being the very first student of Sydney Banks after his enlightenment experience, has an important and riveting story to tell. That is why I am honored to have been allowed to serve as editor for this wonderful work.

Jack Pransky
Boca Raton, FL/Hull, MA
August 2017

AUTHOR'S NOTE

In the midst of an unprecedented heat wave in Western Canada and Saltspring Island just off the Coast of British Columbia, where I still live, I go to the beach for respite. There is none. Here, on the shady side of a secluded beach, where normally the sun does not linger long enough to warm sand and water, even here one cannot escape the inexorable heat.

So I sit, hot, uncomfortable – and out of the past, pictures, events, people, spring up out of nowhere to join each other as I write. It is too hot and sultry to bring my iPad, so I look off into the distance. I watch the little ferry wend its way over from Vancouver Island. Watch young boys splash and scream, and try to capture the random thoughts that will become – are becoming – my story.

Back, back I go in my memory. The tide is flowing in, the waves tumbling, yet they bring no comfort. It is still, hot, humid. I wish I'd brought my swimsuit. Further back I go, and finally, I am back, way back in childhood.

It is a warm day in late summer. I lie in the meadow in front of our semi-rural home on the fringe of a large city on the Canadian prairies. I am six, perhaps seven years old? I lie in the warm grass, long and sere; brown now as autumn approaches. I feel warm and safe.

Suddenly before me, a small movement. It is a wee mouse. She scurries to a small nest made from dry leaves and grasses. Inside are four or five even smaller mice, only an inch or so long. I am mesmerized. I sit and watch. I am filled with a strange and wonderful warm feeling. It is happiness. It is safety. It is love.

Somehow, I am one with the little mousies. With all creation. I believe this to have been my very first experience of "going inside." A something beyond my small self. And so, in thinking back, my search must have begun that day in the meadow. I wanted that feeling back. I wanted it to be with me forever!

And so, the search began. It would be several decades before I would regain something of this feeling, after meeting friend, mentor and spiritual teacher, Sydney Banks...

INTRODUCTION

"I'm not going to be around forever!"

Sydney Banks had dropped in unexpectedly as he often did, for a quick cup of tea. It would be one of his last visits before he passed away in May of 2009.

"Someday," Syd continued, "someone is going to have to tell my story, and you are the only one who can do it!"

For once in my life I was speechless! Shocked, that after leaving Syd's teachings more than thirty years before, he would choose me. So many people had stood by Syd all those years, and I was not one of them.

Secondly, I was flattered. Syd had worked with many people over those three decades — psychologists, psychiatrists, therapists. He had lectured in colleges, prisons and universities. Why would he ask a country artisan soapmaker to tell his story?

Third, I was quite intimidated. Syd and I had parted as teacher and student in a not very pleasant way, and I was afraid my version of "his story" would contain things he would not choose.

"Why me?"

But I never asked the question! I was too totally confused and puzzled. I wondered, and still do, what perspective I had that would move him to ask me over others. One of the biggest regrets of my life is that in my flustered state I did not ask Syd to elaborate.

Although Syd and I had worked together almost every day over five years in the 1970s, I had left Syd's teachings and the group of students that surrounded him, and for the next thirty years pursued my own path. Syd, my friend, became Sydney Banks, philosopher and teacher of students, psychologists and others around the globe and had founded The Three Principles, which would culminate in a world-wide movement to disseminate his teachings. Syd apparently had not even told his group of devotees that he kept in touch and remained friends with those of us who had left the group, so they likely had no idea.

Syd's vision and deepest heartfelt desire, I knew, was to help others find the joy and peace he had discovered in one amazing moment in late 1973 when he had become "enlightened." And in 1974, deep in a spiritual quest of my own and seeking an enlightened one to guide me, I had become Syd's first student.

Six years would pass from that day in 2009 and I often pondered Syd's words, when through a strange series of events I finally realized, "I can't tell Syd's story!" I wasn't even around for most of it, nor was I deeply interested in what came to be his growing worldwide Three Principles community. I could only tell my own story, of how I came to meet this strange and wonderful man, of the impact he had on my own life. And in a typically mystical kind of way, which was *always* the way with Syd, as I was coming to this realization I would come in contact with someone who knew someone, and ultimately I was asked to tell my version of Syd's story.

Here is that story...

CHAPTER 1

I MEET A MYSTIC

July 1974. I wake up in The Hollywood. I am completely disoriented.

I don't know who I am, where I am, or what I am doing here.

This is not Hollywood, California. It is The Hollywood Hospital in New Westminster, British Columbia. The infamous Hollywood Sanitarium opened in 1919 as a private hospital to treat "prominent and wealthy members of society including a number of celebrities." These apparently included actor Cary Grant, crooner Andy Williams and Ethyl Kennedy, wife of Robert. None of them appeared during my stay, unfortunately.

In 1959 its name changed. They began experimenting with psychedelic drugs to treat drug and alcohol addiction and personality disorders. Soon they became infamous for being among the first medical hospitals in the world to experiment with LSD. The medical establishment viewed them suspiciously. Thus, The Hollywood was forced to close its doors in 1975, shortly after my stay.

They also specialized in ECT, or electroshock therapy.

To this day, I cannot remember exactly how and why I ended up in The Hollywood. I did not drink, have a drug habit or a "personality disorder." I was simply severely depressed. In deep therapy at The Hollywood they couldn't find any obvious reason for this, so they concluded I must have had a severe trauma in early childhood that I couldn't or didn't choose to recall. I think that means they couldn't figure it out.

Perhaps it had been post-partum depression, as after my son Gary was born in 1966 I changed from the happy, cheerful girl I had been, to become slightly depressed. My doctor in Vancouver gave me medication but that didn't seem to help, so he suggested I see a psychologist, who suggested I get a divorce. So I did. That led to more depression. I felt medication and psychology had failed me, so I joined a succession of strange groups.

At about the third group I met Bill. He, too, had married young and was going through the breakup of his marriage and searching for something. We hit it off, and within months I quit my job, sold my house, and moved to Saltspring[1] Island. We heard rumours that it was a veritable hippie paradise, filled with draft dodgers and communes and we thought, surely, here we would find ourselves.

We bought a cottage in the middle of a forest with a stream running through and a small waterfall. *Very* romantic! I think we may have "lost ourselves," because two months later our relationship ended. Bill left the Island and I found myself in The Hollywood having shock treatments.

One old friend who visited me there at the time said, "What are you doing here? I think you're just here to gather information for a book!" How prophetic! *One Flew Over the Cuckoo's Nest* had recently been published and indeed The Hollywood had its own Nurse Ratched. The

---

[1] The original spelling was Salt Spring Island, but was officially changed to Saltspring Island in 1910. Both versions are currently accepted.

hospital, located in a grand old mansion with vast land-scaped grounds in the middle of a big city, was weird! It had a padded cell. I walked past it one day and looked in. I didn't ever want to go there. I was a model patient.

They administered the maximum number of shock treatments allowed by law in British Columbia. Eight. The problem with having my brain filled with new brain cells, which is what they claim shock treatments do, is I couldn't find my old brain cells! My short-term memory disap-peared, and with it the depression and whatever had been bothering me.

They sent me home from The Hollywood with a stockpile of drugs; six different prescriptions, one a muscle relaxant, one for Valium, some Chlorpromazine, and Thorazine—a kind of chemical straight jacket. I was told I needed to be on these medications for the rest of my life, and I must return for more electroshock treatments every six months for the foreseeable future.

I returned home and collected Gary, now 7 years old, who had been staying at a friend's, and we returned to our cottage in the woods. What would I do now? I pondered the future and it wasn't rosy. My feelings were a strange mixture of relief at being home, fear of the future, confu-sion about what had happened, joy at being home with my young son, excitement at living on a small island and the terror of more shock treatments.

I knew I was seriously seeking something, something nameless I couldn't even articulate. A typical child of the sixties, I was searching for "myself." The Beatles had the Maharishi, and I loved Ram Dass. *Be Here Now* became my Bible.

I checked out the local paper, the *Driftwood*, and found

a notice that a Kundalini Yoga practitioner came to Saltspring every Wednesday and gave lessons. We met at the local courthouse and formed a circle on the grass each week. Our guide, a young American, wore white cotton and a turban. I learned to breathe properly and recite a mantra while doing several other things with my consciousness. It was fun and exciting, and so New Age, but I walked away each week feeling vaguely dumb and disoriented.

The next week I noticed another ad in the *Driftwood*.

"For anyone seeking guidance through self-awareness I am offering an informal friendly type group situation based on the here and now. This group will be led by someone who himself is enlightened."[2]

Fascinating! I had been reading books by "enlightened" men and had read repeatedly that "the moment a student is ready, the guru will appear." I was ready! Would he appear?

I called the number listed. Soon I was speaking to a friendly man with a strong Scottish brogue. He invited me to come over and talk.

The next day I drove a mile or so up the road, turned into a long winding driveway and up to a small white cottage set close to the sea in a lovely meadow bordered by huge firs.

I knocked. A petit woman with a warm smile greeted me. A man dressed casually in jeans and a blue shirt came to the door.

---

[2] *The Driftwood*, August 28, 1974

"Come in," he said. "I'm Sydney Banks. Would you like a cup of tea?"

Syd and Barb

CHAPTER 2

WHERE TO START?

At The Hollywood, we each spend an hour a week with the psychiatrist who happens to own it. He tells me I have an irreversible trauma, perhaps from early childhood, too early for me to bring to conscious memory in therapy sessions. But he makes me go back through my life.

Memories come flooding back.

As a child, I was very precocious and just loved to read. I haunted the local library and had my sister check out books for me, as under Grade 3 we were limited to *one book*! After that, we could check out three! Whee! I read mostly, perhaps only, fairy tales. The Red Book of Fairy Tales. The Blue Book of Fairy Tales. The Brothers Grimm. I was fascinated by the idea that there were small invisible beings around, and walking to school through the woods I could almost see them. Fairies, gnomes and elves; they seemed more real to me than my friends at school.

By ten or twelve, my interests changed. I no longer believed in the little people, but had discovered — aliens! Not for real. Every Saturday my big sister took me to the movies, and I must have seen every Roy Rogers and Gene Autry movie ever made. Westerns bored me, but this was the early fifties: *The Day the Earth Stood Still; The Man from Planet X*! I can still see his scary face looking through that window. I was fascinated. On cold winter nights walking home from the skating rink I watched the brilliant clear and cold night sky, knowing any moment I would see something move amongst the bright drift of stars—and I knew they were coming for me. I was one of them.

My psychiatrist pressed. Not the memories he is looking for. Okay. My father has had a bad car accident, has a broken leg and hip and is unable to work. Dad is drinking, and home has become a scary place, with much yelling and way too much discipline. Mom is trying to cope with it all; four kids and a huge garden.

Perhaps it was the twelve years I spent in Catholic convent school? Forced to attend church on Sundays, I hated the long walk, the formality. I had to go to confession every week and reveal I had smacked my little brother, then do penance for it. I rejected all the rules and refused to feel guilty about my youthful "sins." Yet, I loved the pageantry, the incense, the robes and statues and finally the moment of silence when the Host became present. Looking back, I feel in some of those moments that I actually experienced something the priests and sisters called "God." It was, certainly, "the Peace that Passeth understanding." Somewhere in my life, I had not only lost that peace, I was flung into almost literal Hell. My life had become unbearable.

Had I ever been sexually abused by a priest?

"No," I told the inquisitive psychiatrist, but I had been slapped around a bit by different nuns. I had Mother Mary Alice for typing class. We called her "Nightmare Alice" as she was so big, tall and intimidating in the black habit she wore. One day during class when I apparently looked at my fingers while typing, she came up behind me and rapped my fingers harshly with her pointer, almost breaking several.

Later, when I married a Protestant boy I was excommunicated, and that was that.

By my late teens, I had discovered physic phenomena, reading *Psychic Discoveries Behind the Iron Curtain*. I watched on T.V. as Uri Geller bent spoons with his mind. I sure was impressed. I tried it, too, but it didn't work, and they later said he was a fraud. I read everything I could find about mental telepathy, ESP and the paranormal. I was obsessed with the idea that there was something...more. Some secret we weren't being told.

I was a good student, but in high school I lost interest in my studies when I made a startling discovery. Boys! My father, a strict German disciplinarian like his father before him, decided I was too young for boys. I wasn't allowed out on weeknights, and on weekends had a 10 o'clock curfew. Just enough time to attend a high-school football game, but not enough for an exciting ride to the A&W later.

Soon I was always in trouble. Always late coming home from school, staying out past curfew, lots of phone calls with my silly girlfriends. I think Dad felt he was losing his grip. One night I came home very late with a boy loitering on the sidewalk outside. Dad met me at the door. Perhaps he had been drinking again. He stepped towards me, yelling loudly and I panicked! Out I went, into the street and home with the boy who would become my future husband.

Mom tried to patch things up, but it didn't work. I moved in with my older brother Larry and his wife and continued with Grade 12. Soon, they moved away and I just went out and got an office job and a room of my own. Two months from graduation and an honour student, there I was, out in the big wide world. I now had an engagement ring, and on my eighteenth birthday, got married in a small civil ceremony.

In 1965 Ron and I moved to Vancouver and I did office work, moving upwards until I was Executive Assistant for a big mover and shaker in the Vancouver business community. I hobnobbed with the mayor's secretary, the top stewardess' at Air Canada and others who belonged to an elite group of women in business. Then, in 1966 little Gary arrived and my life changed.

After a couple of years at home, baking, cleaning, washing dishes, I became ill and depressed. A kindly doctor suggested I should go back to work, so I did. But those years at home gave me more time to read even more books, do even more searching. I think now part of my restlessness was a kind of "existential angst," for I had lost direction in my life.

Many of us had been conditioned, I believe, to follow that dream, to find that handsome prince, to have a wonderful, happy, healthy child, to buy a new home in the 'burbs. I even had a fast, new convertible to drive to work. At age 25 I felt I had succeeded in achieving the American Dream—actually the Canadian Dream. I had everything it took my parents thirty or forty years of marriage to achieve.

As I became more and more depressed my doctor gave me a mild tranquillizer. Didn't work. Sent me to the psychologist who after a few weeks of therapy said I needed to get a divorce. Well, things weren't going well in my marriage either, so I followed her advice. I felt even more depressed. I was getting desperate. I did a lot of partying now with my friends from the office, but as time went on it only made me feel worse and worse. It was all so pointless!

CHAPTER 3

CRAZY THERAPIES

In the midst of my growing ennui, a flyer arrived from our local community college for their night school courses. I can't remember how they billed it, but I joined a group interested in ESP, and they talked a lot about Eckankar and out-of-the-body experiences. Right up my alley! I kept practicing and one night awoke to find myself standing in the closet watching myself asleep in bed. Terrified, I decided this was not for me.

The next class I joined was better, and after an hour or so of talk they had a meditation. Had never heard of it. But—something happened. I sat for that half hour and was neither awake nor asleep, but something in between. I believe I went into a deep state of meditation because the next day I awoke to a feeling of well-being that had escaped me for years.

The next semester, the College offered an Encounter Group. At the office, the Branch Manager, the Sales Manager and a few others were sent by Head Office to one of these groups. Apparently they learned to communicate better, to face their fears. So, off I went. A sociologist and a psychologist from the college taught a very exciting night school course using what I now know were "Crazy Therapies."[3]

The first evening with the lights turned off we were to

---

[3] *CRAZY THERAPIES: What Are They? Do They Work?* 1996. Margaret Thaler Singer & Janji Lalich

mill around in the darkness, giving each person we met/felt/bumped into a hug. This would make us more open and trusting of each other. Later, Bill told me the guys thought they had died and gone to heaven. I remember a couple of "hugs" that made me a bit uncomfortable.

Another time we were to choose partners for a massage. I was chosen by one of the facilitators, an older married man with children. When I refused to disrobe for the massage he humiliated me in front of the whole group. We had all discussed our backgrounds, and it seems I was horribly repressed from my years at the convent school and had a lot of "false modesty." At 25 I didn't want to point out that a 50 year-old groping me was actually kind of creepy. Besides, he was in charge!

As winter progressed, more couples sat airing their grievances, other groupies just disappeared and we got into the really "Crazy Therapies." They practiced Primal Scream and other questionable "therapies" our facilitators had learned from books.

They had "hate sticks" and we were encouraged to grab one and hit the pillows every time an issue came up. Once, under prodding, I said my Dad was mean when he drank. My turn at the pillow. "So, how did THAT make you feel?" I wasn't sure. It had happened so long ago. But, after fifteen minutes beating the pillow with the stick I knew it had wounded me deeply.

Then, "Where was your mother when all this was happening?" Well, I thought, probably washing clothes or cooking. But no, it meant she wasn't there for me, either. More pillow beating.

My mother was one of the kindest and most compassionate people I have ever known. Once a tramp

12

wandered over from the railroad tracks in our area. Mom was hanging clothes out on the line on a lovely spring day, and I was playing nearby. The ragged fellow came into the backyard and asked if he might have a bite to eat. Mom welcomed him in like an old friend, took out bacon and eggs, homemade bread and made him a robust meal. I never thought about this for thirty or forty years, but I do not fear the homeless and don't mind feeding them either. Mom was a Saint. And here I was beating a pillow and yelling at her for mistreating me!

Others in the group had the same kind of experiences and sometimes we shared these outside of the college room where we met. Some of us became very close friends, for we shared so much we had never spoken of to anyone. But, as the confrontations and animosity grew, we were encouraged to tell each other off. "You talk too much!" "You're just a Big Ego!" and so on. The quietest among us, a married lady whose husband had had an affair, was told to shut up, because whenever she talked, "she whined!" Some of us hated each other, the couples all yelled and screamed and were encouraged to "let it all out!" Not a good idea. Children were involved. Each and every couple split up, without exception.

After a few months of this, we were making too much noise for the other night school groups, so we left the college and met in private homes, including mine. Then we began weekends where we would pay our leader and stay overnight together. That was interesting! None of this made me feel any better. In fact, it seemed I had problems and neuroses I'd never dreamed of, like everyone else there.

Decades later, reading *Crazy Therapies*, where people like us committed suicide, were physically, emotionally and sexually assaulted, all in the name of mental health, I understood at a much deeper level how my experience had helped pave my way into The Hollywood.

But I had met Bill, and we began a relationship after his marriage failed. It was a time of highs and lows. We were both into telling each other off a lot, letting it all out! We had become convinced this kind of brutal honesty was the only way to have a great relationship. Of course, our fearless leader's marriage also collapsed.

One thing Bill and I had in common besides love and lust was a sincere desire to "find ourselves." One thing that drew us together was we were both reading Lob sang Rampa. He talked a lot about The Third Eye. That was *so* cool. Now, instead of fairies, aliens or spoon-bending, we were headed in the right direction: The Spiritual Life. Lob sang apparently channeled a Tibetan Lama, and we found his words uplifting and inspiring after Primal Scream. One of my old boyfriends scoffed, and told me Lob sang was actually a postman from Brighton, England writing under a pen name. I was furious. What did he know? Lob sang went on to write about eighteen books, and was really a plumber from Devon, England. One of his books was purportedly channeled by his Siamese cat. Oh well, nobody's perfect! Routed out of England as a charlatan, he settled, where else? In Calgary, Alberta, where I had lived for years. So much for Lob sang.

Then we discovered *Be Here Now*, which would change our lives. For Bill and me it became daily reading. We followed its practices devoutly and sincerely looked upon it as our "Bible." Apparently, we were not the only ones.

Finally, we were on the right path. Bill had by now

morphed into a "hippie" with a long ponytail and a long black beard. He wore leather clothes and smoked strange things. He was working in a boat-building yard with an American draft dodger, who introduced him to all kinds of new ideas, including marijuana and not working. So Bill quit his job and began making canoes in his back yard. Soon, my new friends were laughing at me for being so "straight," as in having a steady job in an office, wearing high heels, and taking Gary to McDonalds for treats on Saturday.

One day we visited Bill's parents who lived on a large acreage just outside of metro-Vancouver. That Sunday we walked through the countryside nearby and encountered a vacant farm. The old house was falling down, but lilacs still bloomed in the yard, and we could see where a garden once was. Bill and I had been together for about five months and together we began to reject everything about our lifestyles. That evening, lounging in front of the fireplace, we made a brilliant decision.

We would move to the country, go "back-to-the-land" as many of our Woodstock generation did. We would grow our own food and seek peace and tranquility. I had heard of The Gulf Islands, but had never visited them. Bill told me of an island he had heard about. His mother Faye told him they grew nut trees there. Lots of nuts. As Bill described this special place something warm and mystical occurred. Saltspring Island. Yes! I said, "Let's move there!" And we did.

Soon, we listed my nice house in the 'burbs for sale, and Bill and I arranged to meet a realtor from Vancouver on the ferry and we would search for a suitable house on Saltspring Island. John, the realtor, said he would wear a red tie and we would recognize him on the boat, and we did.

John drove us around the magical Island. Breathtaking. He drove us to the little town of Ganges, named after the HMS Ganges, a British warship. He parked at the local real estate office and promptly came out with an older gentleman. This man, Burt, took one look at Bill's long hair and beard, his jeans with embroidered trees, hearts and lightning bolts (made them myself) and my long skirts and tie-dye and drove us down a winding country road; Rainbow Road. How romantic, I thought. I had a cat named Rainbow.

We came to an area of large trees, shaded by a small mountain. Coming down the driveway I held my breath. It was December, and raining. A creek tumbled down the mountain, under the road, and throughout the two-acre property. Down a bit in the woods at the bottom of the lot was a small waterfall with Maiden Hair ferns growing alongside. The house was a small cottage with a large deck out back facing into the huge Douglas firs that grew there.

A squirrel ran up a tree. Ferns waved in the breeze. "We'll take it!"

Later, after we had signed some papers and on the way home, I asked Bill, "Do you remember if it had a laundry room?" Well, it did, but the house was pretty small and basic. I quit my job and we moved in the following March. It was heady and romantic beyond words. But it rained. Every day. I kept waiting for the sun to shine, to admire the countryside, but it was just drip, drip, drip every day from the tall firs.

Gary went to school each day, caught a school bus outside, and Bill and I were left to, well, what? I baked, made cookies. I had recently taken up pottery and made some pots out on the deck where my wheel was. Bill kind of hung around, getting bored and started to visit Vancouver to see his family. These visits came more and more often, and we would argue when he got home.

Drip, drip, drip. April, May. Not even six feet of soil to have a garden. Back to the land? I guess we were too naïve. Turns out this was an all-time record for rain on Saltspring Island. One day, after a prolonged trip back to the city, Bill announced he had a job working with his friend's really bad rock and roll band. He packed up his clothes and left.

So every day I packed a lunch for Gary, got him off to school and sat there watching it drip. I drank about six cups of coffee a day, complete with two or three spoonfuls of sugar, as I had for years at my office job. I didn't realize how jumpy and anxious I had become. The rest of the time I was just really, deeply depressed. So much for the dream.

I visited a local doctor, just starting out in practice. He gave me some mild tranquillizers and tried to help. Decades later, he told me he, too, was going through a crisis at the time, same thing, and he didn't know how to help me. I went back to Vancouver and talked to a lady at a crisis center. She kind of shrugged me off. Visited my old doctor there, who sent me right to the psychiatrist.

After an hour of talking, the kindly psychiatrist gave me some medication and suggested that as my depression had now gone on for years I needed more help. Under sedation, I apparently signed myself up for some therapy and a series of shock treatments. I woke up in The Hollywood!

Bill and Linda as hippies

CHAPTER 4

SYD AWAKENS

"Would you like a cup of tea?" said the smiling man at the door. I had met Barb a few moments before, a lovely quiet woman, and a couple of pre-teens, Susan and David.

On entering the living room of that Olde English style small, rustic white cottage I became completely entranced. Windows covered one whole wall of the room, which took up half the house. Spectacular views! Waves washed upon the shore a short distance away. Even now, in memory, I can hear the constant, slow splash, splash as the waves came in and out, louder with the incoming tide.

Over the next five or six years I would spend hundreds of hours in this room. Some of the most amazing experiences of my life took place here.

Off in the distance were several islands, even smaller than ours. In between, a flow of boats passed in front of our view; some small kayaks with a sole paddler, some small fishing boats, trolling rods held high, which we no longer see. Occasionally, a huge freighter, bound for Vancouver or Japan would roll by.

Syd offered me a comfortable chair looking out to sea and he sat nearby, while we introduced ourselves and enjoyed our cup of tea. Syd began to tell me about his experience. Soon he sat cross-legged before the fireplace which faced the sea. Syd's story was quite unbelievable! It was here that his amazing experience had actually taken place. I was mesmerized, and although after more than four decades I cannot remember his exact words, I remember hearing it this way:

Syd and Barb, like so many of us then, had entered the world of "crazy therapies." They began to volunteer at a local crisis center and eventually ended up at Cold Mountain (now Hollyhock Retreat), which had become the center in Western Canada of the personal growth movement. Several months previously they had attended a group there to address some problems in their marriage, which apparently was not going well.

During the weekend, Syd mentioned that he always felt so insecure. He was an immigrant from Scotland. He, in his mid-forties, was already balding and felt self-conscious about it. He was slightly built and took Karate to shore up his confidence. Adopted at birth, he had not had a very happy childhood. Syd quit school at fourteen, ran away to sea and trained as a welder on big freighters which sailed the seas. He was always very conscious of his lack of education and shared his insecurities over and over at the group.

On the last day, while speaking with another participant, as he again told his woeful story, the man looked Syd straight in the eye and said, "There is no such thing as insecurity!"

Syd stood there, stunned. This was not the kind of response he wanted or was used to. On telling his sad story he usually got a lot of sympathy, but not this time. He was speechless, kind of thrown into another world where his usual reality didn't exist. As I recall, it was kind of like, "Well, if I'm not insecure...?"

Syd and Barb retreated to Saltspring Island for a short holiday, where Barb's mother Mary had a small cottage on the water. On the third day, according to Syd's account, which I would hear many, many times and it was always totally enthralling, Syd had a breakthrough. He had been sitting cross-legged in front of the fireplace, pondering again and again the magic words, "There is no such thing as insecurity!"

Syd listened as Barb and Mary talked in the kitchen and, suddenly, he could see the conversation in a whole new light. He saw a whole new reality behind the words he had heard. It was all a vast game, and we are all playing it! He broke out laughing at the profound depth of human unconsciousness, and then, suddenly, he *Knew*! There *is* no such thing as insecurity! He became engulfed by white light! In that second his life changed, and he said, "I'm home!" His experience was complete – his "satori," as Syd used to call it.

Syd walked into the kitchen. The ladies inquired, "What's so funny?" It appeared he was laughing at them, and they were none too amused. He tried to explain what had happened to him.

"I'm home," he kept repeating. "I'm home. I've found the secret to life. I'll be writing books about this!" There was more, but instead of grasping what to Syd was so obvious, so apparent, they became more and more puzzled – and concerned.

As the days passed Syd spoke more and more about his experience to the family. Mary and Barb, Barb's brother Dave and his wife Carol, and especially Barb's oldest brother, who was a surgeon at a big city hospital, all believed that Syd had kind of "lost it." There was talk of taking him to EMI – the Eric Martin Institute – the mental facility in Victoria, British Columbia.

Syd wanted to tell about his experience to all the friends and acquaintances who had been part of their encounter group or were at all interested in "consciousness raising," such a prominent movement at the time. He never doubted for a moment that they would be astounded to hear of his recent experience and eager to hear his message.

They were not. Some were openly hostile, he told me. Others just didn't get it. Still others thought he must be on LSD. Over time, I believe, he realized not everyone in the universe is looking for "truth," and he just didn't go there if people were not interested, but initially he wanted to share his blessings with others he cared for, and, he realized, perhaps he had gone overboard.

Later Barb would joke that she, indeed, thought Syd had lost it, but this new, apparently crazy, deranged Syd was so happy, so kind, so easy to get along with that she barely recognized him. He became the perfect husband and father, and Barb would laugh, "If this is crazy, then I'm all for it!" She who knew him best did not doubt he had undergone a major psychological, emotional and spiritual transformation.

Syd shared some of this with me that first day. He recalled how he had gone back to the mill where he worked and had so changed that co-workers barely recognized him. Over time, he spoke with some of them about his experience, that he now knew the secret to life and would speak of the new reality he saw, but they weren't buying it! Syd told me, "They thought I had gone to the fairies," which I'm told is a Scottish way of saying he went nuts.

During this first visit I kept trying to tell Syd about *my* experience; the Hollywood, the drugs, the shock therapy, zapping my brain into Hell! But he wasn't interested. I felt it kind of mean that Syd wasn't listening to *my* sad story, as if the momentous things I had just experienced were not earth-shaking tragic events.

"Oh, well, it's all in the past!" he said. Every time I interrupted his narrative to tell my sad story, he would say something similar. I began to think he had a great big ego and only wanted to talk about himself. Later I would see that he really, really wanted me to "get" what he was talking about, so he could help. But it took me months to realize that by not giving my situation any "energy," as Syd put it, he was really helping me to heal from the events of the past few months.

After a cup of tea and a homemade cookie or two it was time to leave. I had been the only person to reply to Syd's advertisement in the local classifieds, but he desired to form a group of his own, without the confrontational regime that he, I, and so many others had experienced. No pillow beating. Instead, it would be dedicated to Syd speaking and teaching *Truth*, as he then called it, with a group of students like myself who "got it."

Later, I would be asked again and again, "So, how do you know he's enlightened?"

I had never met anyone like Syd in my life. He simply radiated *LOVE*. His eyes shone and twinkled. He was so present at each and every moment, more alive than anyone I had ever known. He was the embodiment of "Be Here Now" and breathed every sense of Enlightenment I had ever read about. Syd was the most quietly charismatic person I had ever known. Just sitting and listening to him speak was mesmerizing.

Syd would talk about his job at the mill, shopping for a new used Chevy or the meaning of life with equal passion. He had the world's most developed sense of humour I had ever experienced. To him, life was now one big joke, and the joke was on us! We all lived in a kind of delusion, he would say, and then explain the delusion to us, such as the delusion that he was insecure, or that I was mentally ill.

Wow! It was all a bit much. That afternoon left me reeling and kind of took my breath away. At the door Syd mentioned he planned to write a book about his experience. I had told him briefly about my recent past and sitting all winter in a small cottage in the West Coast rainforest surrounded by fog with the giant Douglas firs drip, drip, dripping seemed quite daunting, and that I had decided to write a book about my recent experiences.

I will never forget his next words.

"Good," said Sydney Banks. "Then we'll write one together!"

CHAPTER 5

A NEW REALITY

After that first visit the cadence of my days changed drastically. After lunch I would tidy up and make the leisurely drive a couple of miles up the road to the white cottage. Often, I took Gary and he'd spend the afternoon playing with Susie and Dave, as Syd and I, and sometimes Barb, would talk.

Those late summer days of 1974 had a most unreal quality to them. Here, all I'd learned at home, at school, in life, was questioned, disregarded, or simply laid to rest as the new reality evolved. Everything I thought I knew about life, relationships, work, heaven, hell and everything in between was taken from its normal place in my thoughts, feelings and life experience, and put somewhere else.

Whether talking about life, the latest news, the past, present or future, I would hear Syd state ideas that were almost mind-boggling in their simplicity or strangely hallucinogenic in their complexity. This was, indeed, a strange new world.

Things that had seemed of utmost importance in that other world — jobs, career, entertainment, fun — receded into a nether-world, where they became almost something observed from another planet or galaxy. Now, I had to mold my life around new ideas and new philosophies, such as —

The past did not exist. It was not important. We didn't

need to ever think about it! The future did not exist. We could make plans regarding a trip, school, work, but otherwise ignore the future. Live only in the present? Today this notion can be found in many places, but not in 1974.

It's all thought! We can change the world with our thought. What?

I had read *Be Here Now*, memorized it even, along with all those other New Age, spiritual and consciousness-raising books of the era.

Yet, the man sitting before me on the carpet, where he seemed most at home, had me wrap my head around ideas that might have come from Planet X! I would drive home in a kind of swoon. What had happened? What was going on?

I had just come from months and years of sitting with rapt attention with professionals who had spent years, decades perhaps, learning everything about the mind, the emotions and the importance of the past. I had even progressed to one of the most prestigious psychiatrists in the city, spending hours with this wise gentleman in the suit and tie in his large office talking about my past family history. Now, I was sitting on a lawn chair on a small island, looking out to sea, enjoying the afternoon sun, sipping iced tea, while a bearded guy in jeans and a T-shirt told me to forget the past. That I was actually okay—a good mother, intelligent, healthy, and an excellent cook. That my search was over. That I didn't need to learn anything, know anything; I already knew it all. I just had to trust in myself.

Of course I had to wonder if it were he who was deranged. Yet, each day as I travelled back down the road to my little cottage in the woods, I would be happy, laughing, chatting merrily with Gary or Bill. The events of the past years seemed to recede like a bad dream—indeed, had been a bad dream—and now, I had woken up.

In moments, I felt that old familiar tightening in the pit of my stomach—the fear, the insecurity, the dread of another visit to the Hollywood. Yet, as soon as I became aware of that feeling and those thoughts I just told myself it was all in the past and, almost instantly, my thoughts and feelings changed and I was back in the present.

I would visit Syd and Barb's every day or so. At that time none of us were working. It was late summer now, and it seemed we had all the time in the world. We spent endless days sitting in lawn chairs on the vast acres of meadow surrounding the small cottage, looking out to the ever-changing sea.

It all seemed so natural, so normal at the time. But in hindsight, being the first and at the time only serious student of Syd's teachings, so fresh and new after his recent experience, was such an incomprehensible event that even now my mind reels.

Syd did not meditate, as such, and later I would learn he did not agree with movements that "sold" one a mantra to endlessly repeat. One of my old acquaintances from the city said she became so obsessed with her mantra that she couldn't help but focus on it and had to have help and take medication for the mantra to be wiped from her constant thoughts.

Syd, however, did believe in what he later called "the state of meditation," and it seemed he spent most of his time in that state of consciousness. Often, when I drove down the now familiar driveway, he was seated in his favourite chair, usually writing. He would quietly sit by himself and from time to time write down the thoughts and inspirations that came to him, seemingly from nowhere.

These thoughts, I believe, came from what Syd called the "Universal Mind," the Higher Self, and they were always completely and totally incomprehensible to me as he shared them. So, we would talk about whatever it was he'd written. I asked questions and he patiently, over and over again, tried to explain the unexplainable.

He might talk about energy. "It's the energy of all things." So, off my mind went. Energy? Let's see. Like, it's invisible, like energy? It's everywhere, like energy? Or electrical energy, or something like that? On and on my thoughts would swirl, getting nowhere, of course.

Or, even worse, he would say, "It's all an illusion. Just one big cosmic game!" Okay. So, it's like the circus? A trick? Everything we think is there, isn't there? My thoughts just whirled until, in frustration, knowing I would never "get" it, I would simply give up the analyzing and thinking and finally do what Syd always suggested: "Just listen!"

Over time I learned that with Syd's experience had come the knowledge of what God is — not the old gentleman with a beard sitting on a cloud that judged or rewarded us according to our behaviour, but as Syd's in-depth vision had shown him, "the energy of all things." Syd would talk about energy constantly — positive energy and its benefits; negative energy and its pitfalls. It became a huge part of those early teachings.

After these sessions Syd would pass his writings along to me. Neither of us had a clue how we would go about writing a book. Neither of us had ever written anything before. Neither of us had even finished high school.

Yet, everything seemed to flow like a river. The days passed one by one, and slowly we moved into early autumn. I remember two things in particular from that time.

One, coming from my need and anxiety, I still wanted to tell Syd my troubles—the psychologists, psychiatrists, shock treatments and medications. These events seemed pretty shocking to most people. Soon after I returned home from the hospital Bill had come for a visit with an old friend he had worked with in the mill years ago. Vern's new wife came along, a hair-dresser. I mentioned I wanted to do something with my long, straight, boring hippie-hair. Next thing I knew, I sported a freaky-looking Jimi Hendrix Afro. Next time I visited town I headed for the bookshop, one of my favourite hangouts. Just outside the door I ran into one of the amazing older ladies who worked there, whom I absolutely admired and adored. She greeted me warmly and wondered where I had been lately. "Oh, I've been in a mental hospital! I went nuts! See!" I pointed to my Afro. "I just had eight shock treatments!" I thought I would make light of my recent experience—make a joke of it and not get maudlin and tell my sad story.

The lady took one look at me and my hair, turned, and literally ran down the street. I was stunned! I wasn't used to being a mentally ill person. I entered the bookshop and spoke to the other lady who worked there, telling her what had just happened. Beth was wonderful. She shared with me that the other lady was getting on in years and was afraid her eccentricities were bordering on insanity and that she, herself, might be bound for somewhere like

The Hollywood.

"You voiced her greatest fear!" said kindly Beth. "Don't give it a thought! You'll be fine!"

How wonderful people are! Years would pass until I truly realized how strong and powerful her words were, and how the constant, almost daily, input from Syd that I was not mentally ill, that I never had been and was perfectly normal, served to bring me back to a wonderful, happy life.

Years later, volunteering for a local community program working with a group of people with mental problems, I saw that many of them identified only with their issues and problems and being mentally ill. I was amazed, as again and again I realized I had never thought of myself as "a mental patient," either in the past, present or future. What a gift!

What really amazed me was the realization that no one knew what had happened to me, including Syd. He was never interested in the details and how I came to be in his living room. At first, I kept trying, desperately wanting his help. But he wasn't into that kind of help; focusing on my past—not remotely interested. He said things like, "I don't need to know anything about your past to know *everything* about you!"

I also began to realize how harmful all the craziness of those early therapy groups had been. I came to the realization that although I had been seeking in kind of a "dark night of the soul," looking for something meaningful in life besides my new convertible, things had been dredged up out of my past; molehills had been made into mountains. It took me many weeks to figure out what was happening. Each time I tried to tell Syd details of the recent past, he would cut me short and I never once got to tell him the full story. Whenever I began to go there, he would say something like, "Well, that's the past. Would you like another cup of tea, dearie?"

Syd placed so little importance on all that had happened, later I would see it begin to recede in my mind as well. I realized how fortunate I was to have met Syd. I could have spent years, decades even, as some have, wandering through life thinking of myself as a mental patient. I had no idea, previous to this, of the stigma attached to being mentally ill.

Within two weeks of meeting Syd I gathered the six bottles of medication I had come home from the hospital with. I took the antidepressant Elavil, the Valium for anxiety, the muscle relaxant, and the scary Chlorpromazine, an anti-psychotic usually given to treat schizophrenia and sometimes used to restrain violent patients — which I was told by one of the most highly respected psychiatrists anywhere that I would have to take for the rest of my life — dumped the contents out on the kitchen table, mixed them all together, and flushed them down the toilet. Gone. Forever. To this day, I have taken a pain killer or two after a ten-kilometre hike in the local hills or a fifty-eight kilometre bike ride, but never anything stronger.

Soon, I was just another normal housewife. No meds, didn't drink, got up, made the bed, made breakfast, packed Gary a lunch for school, got him off to the school bus, went inside and cleaned the house, did the laundry, and within a few weeks started writing a book with Sydney Banks. Pretty normal.

The other thing I remember with great clarity is Syd quite regularly talked about his experience. It was fascinating, especially to one schooled in the *Be Here Now* enlightenment journey. I believe Syd thought there was something inherently insightful in the words: "There is no such thing as insecurity." I would probably hear them spoken hundreds of times in the next few years.

Syd spoke of the white light and repeated the magic words, "There is no such thing as insecurity," but I never *heard* them in the way he did. For Syd, they were obviously the right words that struck a chord somewhere in his psyche, his consciousness, but they didn't work for me. Yet, no matter how many times I heard them, there was such a light in Syd's eyes, such compelling passion in his voice, such a radiance coming forth, that I would sit mesmerized each time.

In between the hours of Syd speaking and I listening, other times were filled with joking and laughter. Syd recounted the stories of his two near-death experiences. One of these found Syd walking over the Capilano Suspension Bridge in North Vancouver, B.C. Not sure what happened but Syd fell and lived to tell about it, unlike many others who did not.

Another experience found Syd driving from the pulp mill he worked at near Nanaimo, B.C. when he went down a dip in the road. A huge tanker truck filled with chlorine gas had had an accident and the air was filled with toxic and deadly chlorine gas. Syd actually lost consciousness for a minute or two, but somehow managed to drive through and again lived to tell about it.

There were other stories, lots of them, and I have to say that Syd Banks — not Sydney Banks, philosopher and mystic, but Syd Banks, the guy — was the best storyteller I ever met. Syd could laugh at himself in ways others could not, perhaps because he could look at his quirks and idiosyncrasies with a pure and clear light, with no ego in the way. He could see events in a way none of us could; nuances of humour, error, delusion and a whole range of human behaviour in a refreshing and revealing way. Perhaps this is the gift of a man of wisdom.

CHAPTER 6

WE WRITE A BOOK

Early autumn. Occasionally Bill would return for a visit after touring with his rock and roll band. As soon as he came in the door I spoke animatedly about Sydney Banks, my visits, and the book we were just beginning. I imagine my enthusiasm was catchy, because Bill immediately wanted to meet Syd, so on my next visit Bill came with me. Syd, of course, made Bill as welcome as I. Now there were two students!

Bill brought a whole new set of questions. Again Syd would patiently answer. As with myself, he refused to get into any negativity, the past, or anyone's issues or problems. I think because Bill and I had years behind us of "crazy therapy" consciousness-raising, we felt that the past was where the answers lie. If we could only resolve each and every issue from the entirety of our past lives, somehow we would be whole and happy.

Recently, for this book, I asked Bill to share his first impressions of Syd. He was more than delighted! Bill began:

I had encouraged Linda to sell her house and move with me to Saltspring Island, but the life of bliss I imagined did not happen. Not working did not suit me; I had never in my life done nothing.

I soon kind of freaked out, as we called it in those days, and ran away to join a rock 'n roll band. Just like the song said. That was hardly as exciting as I imagined either —

eating a lot of junk food and washing out your shorts and socks in the bathroom sink of a cheap motel each night on the road. And "the road" didn't lead to San Francisco or L.A., but to Kamloops and Blue River.

I returned as often as I could to visit Linda, and although we had broken up I still had strong feelings for her and wished somehow we could make it together. On one of my visits Linda told me about meeting an "enlightened man," and I was excited but cynical.

I met Syd, and relaxed. He was warm, friendly and personable, and as I listened to him it resonated with me. It was really exciting, but I found myself waiting for him to do or say something that I believed would show him to be a phony, an ego. I guess it was too much Lob sang Rampa! I was looking for him to want money, power, sex or something, but he didn't ever disappoint me. Syd just gave love unconditionally; a river of it flowed from him.

I remember asking him, "How do I know the truth?"

Syd replied, "You know the truth when you hear it, because it is the truth!" I will always remember that. It was the first time I recognized what "going inside" myself is.

As Bill told his story and I typed it out I think we were both kind of surprised at what he remembered and the passion and feeling it engendered in us both. Took us back in time to those early days. A lovely moment. We talked more about those early days.

Syd was very patient with us, but occasionally he would become a little sterner than his usual smiling self.

"Just cut it out!" he might say, when one of us tried for the umpteenth time to tell one of our sad stories. "That's just the past. Forget it! Just drop that trip! It's not where the answers lie!" and so on.

We, of course, didn't like his methods, which didn't focus on ourselves and our little problems, but rather, he was giving us a grander, broader view.

Most thrilling of all, Syd and I began writing our book. I would call it *Island of Knowledge*, which seemed so appropriate. I didn't know this was a phrase already used by a famous American preacher, Bockman, back in the '60s. It just seemed to me at the time that the center of wisdom, knowledge and intelligence in the universe must be on North End Road on Saltspring Island.

I am at a loss as to how we accomplished it. It was such an organic, natural process and it just seemed to happen all on its own. I did not take notes. I will always remember coming down that long drive, that endless summer, and seeing Sydney Banks casually sitting on his favourite lawn chair out in the meadow, often just looking out to sea, contemplating; other times writing the way he always did, in pen or pencil on the lined yellow pads from the stationery store.

In his quiet moments Syd would always jot down his inspirations, ideas, and epiphanies and as he often told me, he wasn't thinking them up. They came to him from what he called "the Divine Intelligence," his Higher Self. Excitedly, he could not wait to share his latest break-through, for as he sat quietly in his "state of meditation" these things just poured through him, which he, too, was hearing for the first time, as he often said. He would quickly write down these new and amazing insights and, after we spent hours or days discussing them, he handed them to me for inclusion in the book.

* * *

Syd, Barb, Mary and the kids led a very quiet life. Almost no one visited, except Barb's brother Dave and his wife Carol. They, too, were kind of long-hairs who had "dropped out." Dave later became a computer engineer; Carol had been a nurse. They had four small children. They were very friendly to Bill and me, and soon we were invited over to their home, a small white cottage sitting near the tall and traditional white lighthouse on Mayne Island that sits to this day overlooking turbulent Active Pass.

At first I think they were a bit surprised to see me there. They, too, joked about Syd's experience, and the family discussions about whether Syd should be sent off to the E.M.I. I felt they were a bit amused perhaps by some of Syd's talks, but they sat with us often; Syd speaking, answering my endless questions. I think they became more than curious, and as the days went on I felt they were awarding Syd much more respect, perhaps that he actually had a real student, and it must have startled them that it was a patient from a mental hospital recovering from shock therapy.

Dave and Carol began to visit much more often, and soon, we began to sit together in that room on Friday nights. Now we were four!

Listening to the tide rolling in and out, listening to Syd with always a new and mindboggling notion to throw at us, I felt—and Syd would later confirm this—that the five of us sitting there, quietly spellbound, awaiting each new word with the utmost silence, was the catalyst that drew these new and radical teachings forth. By then, I do not think any of us doubted we were sitting at the feet of a

Master.

Slowly at first, hesitantly, the book began to take shape. At some magical moment Syd and I seemed to hit our stride, and the words came pouring forth from his pen onto the yellow sheets of paper, then unto the old Selectric typewriter I had brought with me from my past life as an executive assistant. Those years of taking notes, capturing those executive decisions about the transportation and mining industry in B.C., all of that mundane and sometimes quite boring work gave me skills that would enable me to work that way with Syd.

I somehow found a way, not only to capture his words, which were actually written down by him and handed to me, but a way to also capture the feeling, the atmosphere, the constant amazement at what I was reading and hearing. Wisdom that I felt perhaps had not been brought forth in such a way since Jesus, or the Buddha, or the later Christian mystics I had read.

The strategy we developed soon evolved into an exciting routine that really worked. I would appear and Syd would hand me his latest musings and thoughts on those yellow sheets. I would read it over, then begin the endless questions. "What do you mean by this?" and "What do you mean by that?" Some days the writings continued the ideas and concepts we had discussed at our last working session. Other times the words I read made no sense whatever; they explored lines of thought that had no context in my life up to then, or exploded long-held beliefs I cherished and guided my life by.

Syd and I would discuss the written pages endlessly, and when next we met with our little group on Fridays we would read and reread the pages and again discuss them endlessly, with Syd listening patiently and quietly. Then, always after a moment's deep thought and sometimes a long, vibrant pause full of the deepest contemplation on his part and almost unbearable anticipation on our part, never knowing what might come through, he would quietly respond.

CHAPTER 7

NEW FRIENDS ARRIVE

With Dave and Carol visiting from Mayne Island almost every Friday night, soon the ritual evolved that would continue for many years. Each Friday night we would gather at the Banks' home and never knew what would take place. Syd and Barb were the world's best hosts, and we were all made to feel welcome and as though we were best-ever friends. Bill and I never failed to be there.

For some strange reason Bill decided that perhaps the life of a rock and roll roadie in a small band was not the life for him, and he began to settle down on Saltspring. To support our rather simple hippie lifestyle he did odd jobs, although I continued to stay at home, making cookies for Gary's lunchbox, dusting spiders from under the bed and getting used to living in the midst of the Pacific Coast rainforest.

Most days I would spend some time working on the book, so I no longer worried about the dripping winter days, but rather looked forward with great anticipation to those long slow days when we would have even more time listening to Syd and enjoying the long Friday evenings.

So, for weeks and weeks we sat around the fireplace, or on warm nights arranged ourselves to look out to the ever-changing vista of the sea. One Friday evening we arrived to find a strange car in the driveway. Inside, we were introduced to a new couple, Pam and Jim Beck. They looked vaguely familiar and it seemed we had sat through a long, midnight ferry ride together recently.

Pam had a very British accent and a smile that lit up any room. Jim Beck was a handsome dude, quieter than some of us, and it appeared they met Syd purely by accident, talked for a while and decided that, yes, they would love to join our little group. Now we were six.

Over forty years later Pam and Jim would still be in our lives, minds and hearts, and the journey we shared together would change all of our lives forever. Recently Pam passed away, and the hours I spent with her in the last days were some of the most inspiring times of my life. Not for a moment did she despair over or mention her illness, nor ever express a second of self-pity or sadness. Her only concern was the family she left behind; Jim and their three children and the grandchildren. I can still hear her infectious laughter and see her radiant smile. Together, Pam and Jim would add another dimension to our Fridays, and soon, they were an important part of our lives. They had both been teachers, and like Bill and I had dropped out of mainstream society to live a simple country life and raise our children at the beach or in the woods. Not as idyllic as we had all hoped, however.

The addition of Pam and Jim to our group transformed it in many ways. Now, Syd had not only one young person as an avid student but, indeed, the small group he had envisioned when moving to Saltspring. Somehow, this made him a legitimate teacher in my eyes, not just someone I had met who gave good advice. Also, Pam and Jim were not only intelligent and educated but "with it" in a very New Age way, which I admired tremendously.

Years later, when our group grew too large for Syd's living room, and he also wanted us to "share" in a more public way, Pam was chosen to lead our small group. I always believed it was her experience as a school teacher that enabled her to speak and moderate this event in such a professional manner. The following ad appeared in the *Gulf Islands Driftwood*, January 1977:

> *Public gatherings are being held every Friday night at the United Church Hall at 8pm to share the teachings of Sydney Banks, an enlightened man, about our divine consciousness. Donation of $1 requested.*

Recently, I interviewed Jim for this book. I asked him for forgotten details on how, where and when they had met Sydney Banks. Here, in Jim Beck's own words, is that amazing part of the early history:

> *I first saw Syd on the ferry from Vancouver. I was hitchhiking home, and Syd picked me up. Pam and I, a year before we met Syd, were in a situation where our marriage was in jeopardy and we decided to sell our house in Edmonton and move anywhere else.*
>
> *We bought tickets to Victoria, and within two weeks had bought a piece of land on Saltspring Island, a place we had never heard of. Six months later we were living with our two children in a half-finished ramshackle house; plumbing was a garden hose and an outhouse. Wiring was a hundred foot extension cord from our next-door neighbour, and we were broke.*
>
> *I decided to travel to Vancouver in search of financing to finish the house, sell it and move on. The problems that we had fled the city to escape had somehow reappeared. This was one of the lowest points in my life. On the journey over, I took that tentative look over the side, then pulled back.*

Then, I found myself heading home empty-handed on that late night ferry.

I walked the decks for most of the long three-hour journey and searched the faces for some sort of human contact, which I could not find. About two-thirds of the way through the journey we took on passengers at Mayne Island. There were some new faces that I passed on my rounds. I entered the front passenger lounge and stopped in my tracks for a moment.

I was looking from behind at a tired couple sitting in the front row. I was struck by an outstanding sight. These two tired souls, heads bent together, exuded an aura of love. I was temporarily snapped out of myself and walked deliberately forward to get a better look at this quiet demonstration of love. Then I moved on and on the next round, I stopped and took a seat by a group of people on their way to Saltspring.

Here was a couple I would meet again, Linda Quiring and Bill Goddu. I sat beside them for the rest of the journey. The boat arrived at Long Harbour shortly before midnight and I walked into the last pool of light in the parking lot and stuck out my thumb, hoping for a ride. A rather battered old Chevy pickup pulled over and the passenger door opened. Inside, I was about to meet that same couple I had seen earlier and they were to become two of our greatest friends and our great mentor: Sydney and Barb Banks.

This weary couple immediately started sharing, asking after me and giving me complete non-judgmental understanding. They became interested in me, offering encouragement and suggesting that positive solutions might be available. I don't know what it was that was so inspirational, but when we arrived at my dark driveway I insisted they come up to my home so we could speak further. They came!

We awoke my wife Pam. In spite of her surprise at meeting strangers at this dark hour and knowing my mission had failed, she welcomed Syd and Barb and I lit the gas-fired lamp that only shed a dim halo of light. We sat in our little living room and Syd began to speak. Who knows what he said? I remember terms like levels of consciousness, enlightenment, satori, pure truth and other esoteric terms that were foreign then but became familiar as we grew.

Syd and Barb told us that they had only recently moved to Saltspring. Syd said that Barb was concerned about meeting new friends on the Island and thus they were reaching out to Pam and I as potential friends.

Listening to Jim speak, I was taken back again to those magical, mystical days. Who accepts a ride from an old pickup and is soon hearing about higher consciousness? And what might seem an amazing coincidence was of course just destiny waiting for all those involved to come together for the unfathomable experience we shared.

"What do you remember about those first days, Jim?" I asked.

Our first year with Syd proved to be beyond anything we could have dreamed of as "life experience." Imagine, having day-to-day contact with a person who lives pure Truth. Every day I felt ready to burst with the energy that was coursing through me. We truly learned to share on all levels and we experienced the exquisite benefits of hearing and sharing the knowledge that Syd was revealing to us.

At one time I was in a very low space, filled with resentment, jealousy and anger, as though I were at war with the world. It could be described as one of my ego's biggest battles.

Syd had stopped over for a cup of coffee and to see how

we were doing. I wasted no time complaining about the terrible world I was living in and tried to go into detail to justify my illusion.

"Oh, you're just feeling sorry for yourself," said Syd.

"Oh, yeah!" I answered. "What about all this crap I'm going through?"

Syd turned, his eyes blazed. "Why don't you take responsibility for what's going on here? Why don't you take a good look at where you are, right now?"

"Syd, NO!"

Pam tried to intervene, but it was too late. I felt as though a bolt of energy had gone right inside me and touched my deepest core. I was stunned! My whole body was reacting. I looked around at this filthy, grizzled shack with particle board sub-flooring that could never be cleaned, and dusty cobwebs hanging from the beams and a feeling of gloom about the whole place.

Time stood still.

Things were buzzing. I went into a brave, tranquil perception. I saw it all and how it was all my doing.

"He's right!" I said to Pam. "I am responsible for this." Then my ego re-entered the scene for one last gasp.

"I am taking responsibility for this," I growled, "and the first thing I'm going to do is tell you to get the fuck off my land!"

"NO, NO!" cried Pam.

I think Syd smiled slightly, said, "Okay," and went out the door.

"Syd, what's going on?" cried Pam.

"Don't worry, dearie," Syd replied. "He just heard something! Everything is going to change now."

I was so grateful to hear what he had said, as I was already ashamed of my words. Within a week I had apologized to Syd and thanked him for telling me the truth. The cabin was already on its way and I had become a different man. My consciousness had been given a great escalation through the love and understanding of this powerful friend.

I tried to get my breath back! Wow! This was more than I bargained for when I asked Jim if he would like to contribute his memories to this book. I had never heard this story before and was so grateful for the openness and sincerity Jim shared with me and all of us in sharing this experience. This was fascinating! We hadn't talked about the early days in so many years. As we sat in my small office at home, looking out into the old apple orchard, I felt Jim and I had somehow fallen under a spell and had been drawn back together into that unforgettable time. Both of us were left in a quiet silence. I think the telling of it brought back for both of us those amazing, incredible, unforgotten days over four decades before. Words fail me to describe the feeling Jim and I shared that day as we lived again in that magical time, with Sydney Banks, the welder who became the enlightened man, who became the world teacher.

Pam and Jim Beck on ferry to Mayne Island

CHAPTER 8

TIME FLIES

Listening to Sydney Banks, writing a book; suddenly my life had become more than exciting. With Bill's return to Saltspring Island, a new chapter began unfolding in my life. Now Bill, Gary and I had a real home, and Bill put a small ad in the local paper, the *Driftwood,* advertising himself as a home handyman. As we sometimes recalled with a laugh, I think it said something like, "Handyman available. Can do Anything, Almost," or something of the sort.

Life began to fall into a quiet but regular pattern. I was once again a housewife and Bill worked a few days a week building decks for someone or planting tulip bulbs. One couldn't be fussy. Some people didn't like to hire "hippies," although most were impressed with Bill's work ethic. Many years of working in the boat-building industry and on Canada's first submarine had given him good working skills. It seemed on Saltspring that having someone actually show up each day at the required time and do a full day's work was unusual.

I cleaned, dusted, did laundry, and then sat down at my little typewriter to work on the book. Several days a week I would show up at the Banks' home after lunch, and Syd and I would work. Decades later Syd's son Dave would remark that whenever he came home from school, Syd and I would be working away at the kitchen table.

The Friday nights continued and we became good

friends with everyone. It wasn't all just talk about the meaning of life. We all socialized together and shared some of the best times of our lives. Syd especially loved the beach, and little Vesuvius Beach on Saltspring Island is said to be the warmest beach north of San Francisco. Often we would all take dinner down to the beach, the kids swam, and Syd sometimes spoke, sometimes not. It was all very spontaneous and in the moment. We worked together and played together.

Jim Beck:

> *One idyllic day, working on the renovation at Syd's house, we were sharing and thrilled with our work and it must have been when we were starting our Friday nights at the Church and a few of these guys came over to our house on the way home.*

> *All afternoon we smelled this roast cooking in Barb's oven. We went to say good-bye and Barb went to the oven, pulled open the oven door, brought out a sizzling roast beef, and handed it to me to take home for us to share.*

Another fun thing we did, was travel with Syd and Barb often to Vancouver Island, where they had previously lived. Neither Bill nor I had ever visited there, and it opened up a whole new world to us. The beaches at Tofino full of surfers, fishing at Campbell River, hiking the West Coast Trail or visiting world famous Butchart Gardens; for Bill and me it was a world of adventure.

We began to visit the Nanaimo area where Syd and Barb had lived and usually went in my large old Chevy Impala, which could hold about six people. Syd at the time drove an old pickup truck. The four of us would pile into my old Impala and head for the Big Island as we called it.

Syd and Barb took us first to a shop they promised

would be really exciting and that we would love. They called it "The Exclusive" and assured us it was a very up-scale French kind of place. Actually, it was the local thrift shop. Neither Bill nor I had ever visited one before, and I'd always thought it was a place for people to shop who couldn't afford new clothing. Was I in for a treat! Bill dug around in the used tool department, coming up with a shovel or hammer or something that he claimed he'd been searching for forever. I found an English garden trug that I use to this day. On our first visit, when I was still a little not too impressed with the idea, I found a pair of designer jeans. New, they cost about $120 and I couldn't afford them. But here at The Exclusive I found a pair my exact size, looked just like new, and for only $5.00! We were hooked.

Then Syd would usually take us to visit some of their old friends. First, we met Nick and Jean Williams. Nick, I believe, was Syd's supervisor at the Harmac pulp mill where they worked. They were older than Syd and Barb and retired by this time. Later, they would become students of Syd's. But at this point in time, I think all of Syd's old friends kind of looked upon his "enlightenment" experience as flaky, at best. We visited the Williams often, and they were so friendly and kind and obviously loved Syd and Barb. However, I soon noticed that whenever the conversation turned from everyday chatting to Syd's experience, or he talked about how a group of students, including us, had now gathered, there would be a sudden silence.

I felt they were a bit uncomfortable when the conversation turned, and Nick would usually get up and go to prepare tea or something. Jean would sit silently. Bill and I would begin to squirm and want to change the subject. We were rabid to hear Syd speak, but we knew not everyone felt this way. Usually Syd would kind of get it and get back to something more casual, like the weather, the kids or the usual small talk.

Over time, he introduced us to many more people they'd known before Syd's experience. Some of these—Heather and Peter Braun, Sandra Clapham, Sandy and Larry Clarkson, Elsie and Ken Spittle, Jerry Lee and Robin Allen, Richard and Marika Meyer—would become students and move to Saltspring. Elsie would spend decades working with Syd and teaching the Three Principles, into which the teachings later evolved.

By this time Syd started encouraging Bill and I to really share what we were learning and hearing. Things were changing so rapidly for us, we lived in a constant state of excitement. But something made both of us uncomfortable talking about it with strangers, or even to some of the new friends we were making. Later, "sharing" became a major part of the teachings, but neither Bill or I ever felt comfortable doing this.

My way to share was what was happening with the book, which was moving right along and surprising even me with what it contained. I had no idea what it ultimately did contain or what an amazing venture I had become part of. Although we did try to share as best we could, we never wanted to become teachers, and neither of us ever did.

It is important to note that Syd never charged for his time or teachings. I was not surprised. Anyone who truly knew this man and his and Barb's endless generosity would not be surprised. Syd and Barb's home was open to everyone at any time, and somehow they managed to fit us all into their lives. In the beginning, knowing they were not wealthy and that Syd had just quit his job to teach, we insisted on paying for those teachings. We had been in so many groups, had so many teachers by now, that we were used to paying. Syd wouldn't hear of it!

Later, as he began to travel and was asked to speak in different cities, he would of course, accept travel and other expenses. I didn't know how he managed to live, so I just assumed it was Syd's personal assets that became the vehicle for him to disseminate the teachings. Unlike many other famous or successful teachers or "gurus" he did not become a wealthy man from those teachings and never accepted or demanded money from us. Syd insisted again and again that his wisdom, his experience had come to him out of the great openness of the universe. Freely, it had come to him, and freely he must give it out.

CHAPTER 9

THE TEPEE PEOPLE

It was now late fall. The days grew short. We all settled in for a long, dull, grey winter on the Wet Coast. But it was not to be. Bill and I found ourselves enveloped in what must surely have been the most exciting development in the history of human consciousness in Canada: Our very own enlightened man.

Occasionally others would join our Friday group; once, a few friends Bill and I convinced to come for the experience of a lifetime. They were not impressed. I think they thought Bill and I had "lost it." They never returned. Others would join us—friends of Pam and Jim, people Syd met in his daily life and others.

One Friday night, driving through the near darkness now to the Banks' home, we realized the leaves had all turned, the wind blew in huge gusts and the lake looked grey and cold as we drove by. We felt a bit morose, as if those endless days at the beach, the fun shopping trips, that wonderful feeling on Saltspring—"It's *Summer!*"— were fading fast. I felt a bit of anxiety that although my deep depression was truly a thing of the past and only a few months later I could hardly remember that feeling, perhaps dark times would yet return with the darkening of the days.

Driving that long driveway, the wind lashed at the tall trees as we moved closer to the sea. We parked beside the small cottage as we had countless times before. Syd came to the door as usual and greeted us warmly. The slight melancholy I'd felt on the drive evaporated instantly, as he invited us into the living room to meet a new couple. Judy and Jim Wallace would become dear close friends in a relationship that spanned decades.

Along with Pam and Jim, the unbelievable experiences we four couples shared in the coming months were something few people in this lifetime get to experience. We later joked about the twelve disciples, as we followed the Light that was Sydney Banks to a new heaven and earth.

I felt the Wallace's *had* to share their story for this book; theirs was such a critical part. They agreed. No one could enjoy that story more than I, as here in 2016 I relived every detail of their fascinating journey, mesmerized.

Jim Wallace began...

In March 1974 I walked away from seven years of training, five years of practice, a partnership with two very close friends and vowed never to return to practice Law again. I was troubled by stress, anxiety, frustration, alcohol abuse, and a very low opinion of the legal system and my role in it. Judy was expecting our first child and we were desperate to find some way out of the miserable life we were living.

Two years before I left, a client had invited us to spend a weekend on Saltspring Island, one of the Gulf Islands between Vancouver Island and the West Coast of Canada. He took us on a tour of the Island, and we were surprised by our reaction to it. The Island touched us in a way that brought out a release of emotions long forgotten. It seemed to offer a promise of the peace we were seeking so badly. We returned for longer visits and in the end purchased a small acreage within walking distance of the ferry terminal at Long Harbour.

Like many other young people in the early 1970s we believed that the ideal life was lived close to the earth like the pioneers and native Indians had lived in an earlier age. We thought by emulating that lifestyle we would find the peace, health and happiness for ourselves and our unborn child that had eluded us in busy Vancouver.

With the help of The Whole Earth Catalogue we bought a mail order copy of the simplest shelter we could find: a Sioux tepee, and set it up on our land. We spent a lot of time making it as comfortable as possible. At night, with a fire lit, it glowed like a magic lantern. Three months later our son was born there. Rumours that a lawyer was on the Island living in a tepee must have contributed to the local colour, because I actually had a few people come out to our tepee for advice about legal problems. We all wondered how the Law Society would have reacted to the scene.

A few months after that we began to think our beautiful Island was being taken over by urban development and city people. The peaceful life we thought we would find there eluded us again. We started planning to sell the land and buy a live-aboard sailboat, even though neither of us had ever sailed. Something was wrong with our dream but we didn't know what it was.

Then it happened: A seemingly chance encounter that changed our lives forever.

Our nearest neighbour was a local school teacher who was building a log cabin on his land and had hired two builders to hew and construct the log walls. One of them, also named Jim, took a liking to us and came back to see our tepee. Later he brought his wife to meet us. Pam and Jim, with their three kids, became like family to us. This friendship was to have a wonderful effect on our lives; it led directly to our first encounter with the answer we had *sought for so long.*

One day in September that year they all came again to visit, bringing a couple a bit older than all of us, who they introduced as Syd and Barbara Banks. Syd stepped inside the tepee and looked around. "Nice space," he said.

We all sat outside, enjoying the dry heat, shaded by the forest trees. Syd and Barb were unusually quiet; I found myself nervously glancing their way, trying not to stare. In response to something Judy said, Syd began speaking to her in a way that jolted our attention. It sounded like nothing we had ever heard before, about how "thought" and "consciousness" work, spoken in a matter-of-fact way, not quoted from books, as if he understood them perfectly.

When he had finished speaking we sat in silence for a time. Then Syd and Barb invited us over to their home the following Friday evening to share our philosophical views on life.

In the days that followed we went to see Jim and Pam to confirm our impressions of this unusual couple. We speculated that Syd might be an enlightened man, such as we had often read about and longed to meet.

When Friday night came we made our way to Jim and Pam's and drove in their car to the Banks'. The night was alive with a howling windstorm and around a dark bend in the road we came up against a huge fallen tree blocking our path. A dirt road led off to the right and Jim instinctively turned into it. After a few sharp turns, we found ourselves back on the main road heading north to the Banks' with the fallen tree behind us. The road was very dark and it was hard to tell one driveway from the next. Suddenly, Jim said, "I think this is it!" and abruptly swung into a driveway on the right that wound down a grade through a thick forest.

It opened into a clearing and stopped at a small, white house facing a dark expanse of beachfront. Lights in every window and over the back door seemed to welcome us. Syd and Barb came to the door together. They were as calm and quiet as when we last saw them. They ushered us into a warm, bright kitchen, furnished with conventional appliances and a modern-looking dining suite. Their home, from what I could see of it, was as conventional as city houses.

We stepped into the living room. To our left as we entered was an old brick fireplace in which a slow fire burned sleepily. The room was comfortably furnished with sofas and rockers and was full of people. Some were smoking cigarettes, including Syd and Barb, and a smoke haze hung down from the ceiling.

We sat down on a sofa next to the door. Then Syd began to speak. He spoke about an experience he had had the previous year, and how it changed his world from one troubled by stress, anger and conflict to the most beautiful existence he had ever dreamed possible. Then his voice changed and he began speaking the way he spoke to us earlier that week. He related it all to "mind" and "thought" and how they hold the secret to life. The room fell into a strange stillness and no one interrupted him or attempted to speak. He seemed to reach a point where he ran out of words, and after a short pause he asked if anyone had any questions.

Some of those present were openly critical of his views. His answers did not satisfy them. I was surprised when he made no attempt to defend himself or his opinions. A couple of them became angry and argued loudly; eventually they left.

After a few of the guests had departed, someone asked Syd if he was disappointed the way the evening had gone. I

59

was surprised when he said, "yes." He began to explain what he meant, but for the first time that evening I cleared my throat to speak. I leaned forward and in a cracked voice assured Syd that everything was perfect, so there was nothing to be disappointed about.

He looked me full in the eye and said, "It is one thing to say that, but it is another thing entirely to know that it is true!"

I fell back against the sofa as if I had been pushed. His eyes seemed to grip mine and he continued gently talking to me, but my mind was racing. That simple statement had shattered my thoughts so completely I couldn't speak.

Although Judy and I both felt shaken by the events of the evening, by the time we returned home we agreed Syd probably didn't know any more than we did, and although we had been invited back the next Friday we wouldn't be going.

One afternoon, I was waiting with our baby in the warmth of a local restaurant for Judy to finish shopping so we could begin our long trek home before dark. I was getting impatient, but when she arrived she smiled broadly and in an excited whisper said she had just met Syd. She was obviously elated. I asked her to repeat every detail of their conversation.

Bill and Linda, who were at the Banks' home that first Friday night, had continued visiting Syd, and Linda had started a book on their experiences with him. Syd showed Judy a copy of the manuscript and told her to read from page 14. There was a passage, she said, about what happens when you meet a wise person and are not ready to hear what they are saying. You are apt to get into competition with him rather than listen. One part, she said, jumped out at her: "You and your big ego will be the loser."

When I heard that I flushed with guilt. Somehow I knew my fear was stopping me from listening to him. I could see the dramatic change in Judy's mood. She definitely felt energized from her encounter with Syd. But instead of joining her excitement I felt upset by what she told me and felt even more afraid of returning to Syd and Barb's for another visit.

For the next few months we saw little of our friends and assumed a routine of daily trips to Ganges and evening meals around the fire, playing with the baby and reading books on awareness. There was little else to do at that time of year and we spent much of each day just keeping clean and fed.

We did not encounter the Banks' again until shortly before Christmas. Walking in Ganges, we were hailed by Syd from their vehicle. He and Barb and her mother, Mary were on their way to nearby Mayne Island to spend Christmas with relatives.

I walked up to the driver's window and peered in. They all beamed at me with so much warmth it startled me. I felt unable to speak, and I could not avert my eyes. Finally, Syd wished us well and, giving us a significant look, drove off.

Once again, this seemingly innocent meeting left me feeling uncomfortable. But strangely enough, even while I was resisting the feelings that Syd was conveying, we sensed something had happened to us we could not explain even to ourselves.

While visiting Judy's family for the holidays, we were offered an opportunity to take care of a well-furnished home of friends of her parents in North Vancouver while they travelled overseas. The attraction of getting away from the austerity of our island life was almost overwhelming, but we turned it down. We both felt we belonged on Saltspring Island and that we wanted to see the Banks' again...

Jim and Judy Wallace

CHAPTER 10

THE SUN *COMES OUT*

Jim Wallace continues…

On our return to the Island, we joined Jim and Pam at a New Year's Eve party. Pam said they had continued visiting the Banks' and convinced us to join them. The next Friday we drove to the Banks' but once again we had another surprise in store for us.

We arrived at their home just as they were leaving for Vancouver, where Syd had been invited to speak at the New Age Centre on 4th Avenue. They barely noticed us as they said their goodbyes to the family and departed. We stayed and talked with Barb's mother Mary for some time. She was obviously excited that news about Syd was spreading and urged us again and again to go to Vancouver to see him speak publicly for the first time.

The next morning we were still debating whether to take her advice, when we heard the blast from the horn signaling the arrival of the ferry at Long Harbour. In a few minutes it would leave on its return trip to Vancouver. A moment of clarity came to us, as we realized we wanted to be where Syd was speaking. We rushed through the forest to catch the ferry. We were the last foot passengers to make it.

As we entered the cafeteria aboard the ferry, we received another surprise. Jim and Pam had arrived ahead of us. We were thrilled to meet them and embraced them both. None of us were sure where the New Age Centre was, but together we were certain we would find it. When we all stopped at the home of an old friend of theirs in Kitsilano, he knew exactly where it was. We arrived at the Centre early and were surprised to find it packed.

Syd and Barb arrived and made their way to the microphone. Syd appeared very much at ease. He looked in our direction and smiled widely when he saw us. His talk lasted for some time and once again the audience became silent as he spoke and remained so until he asked for questions. It felt like a spell had been broken and people began moving and stretching all at once. There were many questions and Syd laced his answers with humourous stories about Barb and himself that got all of us laughing. Jim and Pam shared some stories of their own. Syd ended his talk with an invitation to anyone interested in finding happiness to come to Saltspring Island. Many of those present took that advice.

From then on, we returned to visiting with Syd and Barb on a weekly basis, first at their home, then as the crowd grew too large for their home, at public halls in communities around south-western B.C. Syd's talks were fascinating! His words made a spiritual connection somewhere inside me that left me feeling elated. His sense of humour was outrageous, and his tales of real events always focused on the unexpected and magical twists that occur during the commonplace moments of life.

But what really stirred us was his ability to explain life; *to talk about God, Spirit and Mind. Not that we could understand him, but the feelings he conveyed when he spoke of "levels of consciousness," "being inside" or "beyond mind" gradually convinced us that somehow we had crossed paths with a very exceptional person. We found ourselves discussing his ideas repeatedly with great excitement.*

That winter had been unusually cold and the few rare

snowfalls were heavy and seemed to stay on the ground for weeks. We had quickly run out of the firewood I had cut the previous summer, so one of my daily chores was to buck up enough wood to keep us warm for another day. I thought I could cut all our firewood by hand, but what I didn't expect was that the work was exhausting and I didn't have the energy to keep up. As the weather worsened Syd offered us the use of a chainsaw, but I didn't want it. I actually believed the vibrations from a chainsaw would remain in the forest to destroy our tranquility for weeks. Syd smiled and assured us that something would happen, although he didn't say what.

We did not have to wait long for the answer; it came with the sudden arrival of a young man, Peter, whom we had met in Vancouver but had not heard from for several years. He had since moved to a town on Vancouver Island. He arrived one day during a snowfall, carrying a chainsaw he had borrowed. Moved by some impulse he did not explain, he had hitch-hiked almost a hundred miles to bring us the saw, without any clear idea where we lived. He stayed long enough to cut us a huge pile of wood and enjoy a meal before rushing away to catch the last ferry. We never saw him again. It was only when I was telling Syd about this later that I realized that I hadn't minded the chainsaw at all.

One wet Saturday afternoon we were visited by a staff photographer from the Vancouver Sun newspaper. He and his family lived across the street from Judy's parents in North Vancouver and we had visited with them at Christmas. He said he was interested in our island lifestyle and said he might come over to see us but didn't say when.

He had brought along a young reporter, and before we knew it we were being photographed and interviewed for a news story. Flattered by this attention I took advantage of the reporter's questions to reiterate my indictment of urban society and the legal system. The reporter must have loved it. We soon appeared as a front-page feature in the paper. I couldn't wait to joke about it with our friends.

My chance came a few days later when we joined Syd and Barb at a local restaurant for coffee. I started to laugh about the story but stopped when I saw Syd wasn't smiling. He looked at me with an expression of disbelief and shook his head.

"You didn't say a word about what's happening to you, about what you've found?" he began. He went on to say that if I couldn't talk about what I had found, then I hadn't found anything!

After they left I felt devastated. I had not noticed how superficial my relationship with these people had been. In the face of undeniable feelings, the insights we were given and the enjoyment they brought to our lives, I had acted as if none of it were true or hadn't actually happened. I saw that my fear of speaking honestly about the changes that were taking place in my life had led to a false and generally negative story about us receiving wide circulation.

All around us, people touched by Syd were changing rapidly and dramatically; many spoke of miracles occurring in their families. The most obvious change to us was in the way our friends who had been listening to Syd looked and behaved. Jim and Pam had definitely become happier and more confident, completely at ease talking about the good things that were happening to them. Not only were the couples finding in each other their perfect mates, their children were affected in positive ways also, becoming quieter, more content and more successful at school. The men talked of how much they enjoyed working and the increased energy *they got from a day's work well done.*

Their excitement reminded me I was one of the few that was not working, and we were running out of money. The work that I was qualified to do, practicing Law, was precisely what I had thought I would never do again after I left Vancouver.

One evening at the Banks' I happened to overhear Syd talking to a man I didn't know (but like me, unemployed) about the line of work the man had been in. It was an ordinary job, one which the man had left for a number of negative reasons. I felt some sympathy for him and expected Syd to as well, but instead Syd described the man's work in a different way. To my amazement, this ordinary everyday job was transformed into an enjoyable opportunity to help others and make a great living at the same time; one that anyone would gladly have as their life's work.

I laughed out loud with surprise, because I saw all that had made the job so attractive was Syd's point-of-view. I waited for an opportunity to speak to him privately and, when I saw him and Barb standing alone together, I reminded Syd of what he had just said. I asked if he thought that one could see a law practice the same way he had described that man's job.

Instantly, they both lit up and turned to me with wide smiles.

"Yes!!" they cried, "that's what we've been trying to tell you!"

From that moment, I knew I would be returning to my profession.

A few weeks later, during a visit at our tepee with the Banks' and a few close friends, Syd remarked that the world remained completely unaware of what was happening on the

Island. After everyone had left, an idea came to me that I had an opportunity to help introduce Syd to a wider audience and at the same time try to counter the negative impression we had created by the Vancouver Sun *story. An opportunity presented itself to me that evening and I penned a letter to our friend, the* Vancouver Sun *reporter. I asked him for a favour: to publish a letter to the editor for me as a follow-up to the story they had published earlier that year.*

Writing the Letter to the Editor was a beautiful experience for me. A feeling of excitement and well-being swept over me as I wrote and the words came to me without effort. The feelings became even more intense when I read it to Judy. The next morning we took it to Ganges intending to mail it, but when we got there, we ran into Jim and Pam in the small park overlooking the town's harbour.

When they heard it, they wanted Syd to see it and before long, the Banks' appeared. When I read it to them, I could barely speak. They listened in silence and smiled when I had finished. They asked me to read it again and again. I found myself listening to my own words. We all went over to our friends, Linda and Bill's, to have it typed.

Several weeks passed before the letter appeared in the Sun. To my surprise, it was printed exactly as written. The editor had given it some prominence on the editorial page, complete with a photo from the earlier interview and a banner headline that read: "Back From Back to the Land." Here are some excerpts from it:

Sir: In early 1975 you published a feature story on my wife, child and I and our experiences living in a tepee on Saltspring Island.

We recently had the good fortune to meet and hear the teachings of Sydney Banks, a resident of Saltspring

Island, a man of such powerful wisdom and insight into the nature of man that he ranks with that handful of men and women who can be described as truly enlightened.

He teaches of peace, personal fulfilment and the destiny of man with such compelling truth that all who hear him are inspired to find within themselves a profound sense of the tranquility and understanding promised by all the world's great religions.

His teachings have had a remarkable and positive effect on myself, my wife and, through us, our young son, as we have learned to share the benefits of understanding ourselves and our fellow man with a clarity we had never dreamed possible. Life-long happiness and contentment, rarely even considered natural in our tension-torn world, are promised all who hear and apply his teachings.

Thousands are finding to their sorrow that happiness and freedom do not lie in merely uprooting one's life-style and going "back to the land," attractive as that may appear. These qualities lie dormant within each of us, and unless we learn to tap the source of love and understanding inside us, thereby erasing all negativity from our lives, we will take our feelings of anger and disillusionment with us and every new lifestyle we attempt will ultimately fail to fulfill us.

We no longer feel the disenchantment with Vancouver and the legal profession that brought us here. In fact, I am returning to the practice of law with the freedom of knowing that happiness and fulfilment have nothing to do with one's occupation, one's lifestyle or anything else in the world around us. They lie "inside" us all.

CHAPTER 11

THE SYDNEY BANKS FOUNDATION

As Jim continued his story event after event flashed into my memory, and I was amazed that he and Judy had remembered those days with such passion and detail. What was most fascinating were all the events and details that I had forgotten, or had never even known about.

Jim Wallace continued:

One afternoon, we met the Banks' while shopping for groceries, and Syd invited us to come to their house for a visit that evening.

We were welcomed into the living room by Barb and found it warm and inviting. A fire burned quietly in the fireplace. A stillness filled the house, but was particularly strong in this room. Everything appeared spotless; the furniture glowed in the soft light.

Syd appeared and spoke quietly about recent events and mutual friends. Barb's mother, Mary, came in from her small guest cottage next to the house. Barb was busy in the kitchen, but joined us from time-to-time bringing us tea, coffee and other treats.

Eventually a change came over Syd; he began to speak as he often had previously, in the mystical manner we loved so much. His voice was extremely quiet; we leaned forward to catch his words. I felt amazed and entranced at the same time. There was something different about this evening; what Syd was saying was completely new but beyond my comprehension. His face glowed with an indescribable,

71

almost Christ-like expression.

Later that evening Syd brought out bedding for Judy and me. He and Barb wished us a warm good night, hugged us both and retired to their room. Judy and I looked at each other. Our faces glowed with colour; we literally buzzed with energy. Then it hit me. The answer I had been seeking for so long was not information; it was a feeling! As we slipped under the blankets, a wonderful feeling of humor bubbled up from deep inside me. I began to chuckle, then laugh, the longest, deepest and loudest laugh of my entire life. I touched a depth of humour I had never known possible and laughed until there was nothing left. I drifted into a dreamless sleep.

The next morning, neither Syd nor Barb mentioned the indescribable talk of the night before. It was as if to them the entire evening had never happened. My curiosity about what I had heard was driving me crazy; the more they talked about everything else, the more I wanted them to talk about last night. I could not believe that they were not as intrigued as I was.

Syd had other things on his mind, for he had noticed a log floating far offshore. He said they make excellent firewood for those quick enough to catch them, and invited me to go after this one. He pointed to a large canoe that a friend had left for his use. Soon we were sculling rapidly out into deep water. The tidal current carried the log away at an amazing speed and it took all my strength to keep up with the pace Syd set for us. The log was huge, too heavy for us to tow, so we let it go. We paddled slowly north along the shore, in the quiet of the early morning. The sudden cry of crows and gulls echoed across the water. A light wind moved the tops of the tall cedars and occasionally rippled the water, but close to shore it was clear and smooth.

I had hoped that once alone together, Syd would acknowledge what I had heard the night before, and I took his silence as a sign that I was about to have some kind of experience that would make it all clear. I felt a strange sense of apprehension and told Syd how I felt.

"Just look at the trees," he said. "Look at the beauty around you. How can you possibly handle any more? Just still your mind and enjoy the day." I had received my first real lesson on dropping the past.

When we returned to the house we found the Banks' family relaxing in front of the fire and we were content to stay with them, sipping coffee and soaking up the tranquility of their home. Syd kept us spellbound for hours, relating one amazing experience after another. Finally, he and Barb wished us well and sent us on our way. We drifted home and into a sleep that lasted until the next day.

Within weeks of our visit to the Banks, we had given up our life as back-to-the-landers, sold our property, moved to a lakefront cabin, and opened a law office in downtown Ganges. It was easy this time. I found that my past beliefs about society, the legal profession and my place in it were only that: beliefs. Beliefs that had caused me more problems than they were worth. Beliefs that had prevented me from enjoying my life.

Most of my legal work came from people attracted to the Island to be close to the energy Syd was generating, as word of his availability began to spread – people wanting to build homes, start businesses, and sink roots in the community. We felt the same way, and within a year, friends in the building trades had completed the most beautiful house we have ever had the pleasure to live in. Our second child, our daughter, was born soon after we moved in.

Beginning with a talk he gave in Courtenay, B.C., Syd agreed to have his formal talks recorded. He found the recording process captured much of the feeling conveyed when hearing him live. But we needed an organization with an office to act as a focus for the enormous number of inquiries and requests flooding unto the Island, and to manage the distribution of cassette tapes of his talks.

A little research confirmed that the best option was to incorporate a charitable Society; an entity that could hold property, distribute Syd's recordings and writings, and act as a contact center for anyone seeking more information about him. Barb chose the name: The Sydney Banks Spiritual Foundation. Although Syd took no part in the Foundation's operations, we named him President, and Barb was Vice-President. I acted as Secretary. The Board met regularly at various locations, which gave me an opportunity to get to know Barb better. I could not begin to imagine how Syd had affected his wife. The calm decisiveness that Barb brought to Foundation meetings would be the envy of any corporate direction, more so because she rarely spoke without her wonderful sense of humor coming out somewhere.

CHAPTER 12

GAMES PEOPLE PLAY

Living on a small island as we do, one would think it nearly impossible to not encounter friends, relatives and acquaintances on a regular basis. Not so. If we don't arrange to meet for coffee, tea, a glass of wine, a hike, a movie, a concert, we may not meet for months and months. So, it was with great delight that I met Sheri Hickman at the Country Grocer. Hadn't seen her for months, perhaps a year or so. We quickly exchanged greetings, and she asked what I had been doing since I retired.

"Writing a book about Syd and the early days. Want to illustrate it?"

We both chuckled. The beautiful butterfly in Chapter VII of my first book, *Island of Knowledge*, and the gorgeous lady after Chapter X were both drawn by Sheri, with no acknowledgement, I might add.

We spoke awhile about the old days, laughing our silly heads off. Although we had known Sheri and Don for decades and our sons Ted and Gary had grown up together, Sheri and Don had left the group early on. On the spot I became inspired to ask Sheri if she would like to share her experiences. Sheri agreed. I was amazed to learn that Syd had kept in touch with Sheri over the years, as he had with so many of us that left "the group." I found her story fascinating and was a bit taken aback as I realized so many people had continued relationships with Syd that I was completely unaware of.

Sheri:

In 1971 after my marriage of ten years ended I moved from the city to Saltspring Island with my three children. I had some idea of "moving back to the land," becoming self-sustaining, and giving my children a country upbringing. I loved the hippie concepts of flowers, peace and love, etc. but worked at a responsible job to support my family.

I grew up in Christianity and even taught Sunday School at one time. Now I was reading Be Here Now *kind of books, but I wasn't really on a spiritual journey. I met Don on Saltspring in 1973 and we began living together.*

One day in the summer of 1975, we went on a picnic with a couple who were in our parents' generation. We had known them for a few years, and on this occasion we noticed a big change in them. They seemed more positive, more real, not bickering so much. I was curious and asked what was going on with them to make them seem happier (nicer to be around) but I didn't say that. They told me they had been to the house of an enlightened man to listen to him speak. Would I like to come? I felt a bit uncomfortable with this idea, and Don was having none of it, but I thought it sounded interesting. It is funny that I took my bag of knitting with me, thinking it might be boring and I'd need something to do. When I arrived at the little house on the edge of the ocean I was greeted by Mary, Syd and Barb. There was a group of about eight other people smiling and friendly.

Syd began to speak. I was so mesmerized I never even opened my bag of knitting! With my mind I couldn't understand what he was saying, so I just let it go and let his words wash over me. I felt relaxed, tranquil and warm inside. He was talking about "fear" and I wondered if he was psychic or something weird because fear was my biggest enemy. How did he know? And he was saying there is nothing to fear but fear itself. I had no idea what that meant, but something inside me went, "That's right! I know that!"

After that, I just wanted to experience those good feelings again, and couldn't get enough of listening to him.

My first realization, to use the language of the '70s, was recognizing my own games. We used the term "games" to describe patterns of behaviour that we used to defend our ego, or sometimes to protect ourselves from being too happy [laughs], as crazy as that sounds.

So, the first time I recognized it, I had this thing that my mom did; maybe it was a pattern that ran in our family. I would be in a bad mood or something and I would pick a fight with Don, and I knew what buttons to push with Don to get a reaction. I would get him right in the middle of it, all defensive, and then I would walk out and slam the door and leave him there, in this frustrated condition.

So, I did this one day. We were building our house and living in a small trailer. So, I started this fight and got to that point of leaving him in his frustration, slammed the door and began walking up Mt. Maxwell. As I walked away, stomping and grumbling to myself, really angry and blaming him, suddenly I was looking down on myself doing this! It was like I really saw this silly little childish game, and I thought how much I loved Don and what a caring, sensitive person he was, and what a cruel thing to do to somebody you love. I turned around and walked back, apologized, gave him a big hug and I never did that again, ever in our relationship. And that is forty years!

Sometime after that, we rented a house while still building our house, when our son Teddy — he was about 12 — would get up in the morning and put on his best shirt and best clothes that were for special occasions, not for school. I would always say, "Teddy! You can't wear that to school, you'll get it dirty!" and we would have an argument about it, and maybe he would change it and maybe he wouldn't, but he would leave upset and I would feel upset and mad at him. So, this one morning he got up and he put on his best shirt and he came into the kitchen and I said my usual thing, "You can't wear that to school, you'll get it dirty!" And he said, "Yes! I probably will!"

It broke the pattern! He broke the pattern! I looked at him in shock and he looked at me and smiled, and we both realized at that moment that we had both broken that pattern. He did it! He knew it. It was like he looked at me and said, "Hey, Mom! We don't have to do this anymore!"

When I talk about changing games it's these simple little everyday patterns that hold you up and keep you in negativity, and changing them just makes you happier, but you have to see it! You have to feel it! You can't just make a list and say, "I'm not going to do this anymore!" It's something that just occurs. The more we listened to Syd and the more we felt our fear, our ego, our defensiveness, the more these things just dropped away.

Sheri and Don, kneeling, at their wedding,
with Syd and Barb and the group
(Linda and Bill were away)

CHAPTER 13

PERSONAL TEACHINGS

As word spread that an enlightened man was living and teaching on Saltspring Island, people were drawn by the aura of energy emanating from him like a veritable magnet. It was a sight to behold.

If you were looking for enlightenment, a change in your life or whatever, Syd dealt with us in a more direct and personal way than it later became. In the beginning there were only eight of us; thus, personal teachings were possible. Later, when there were twenty Syd found doing this almost destroyed his life and family. If he got on this personal level with, say, twenty people, he would get calls night and day. He would hear a constant knocking at his door, with people bringing their personal problems and issues, and I might be one of them.

So Syd put a sudden and drastic stop to this. Natural-ly, when he began to speak to crowds of fifty, one hun-dred and two hundred, he went beyond the personal to the vast complexities of the spiritual world and later into the psychological.

Thinking back, it is really hard to explain. Jim Beck and I discussed this, as did Bill and I and the Wallace's. Again, the teachings that appeared in the books we wrote together were initiated by Syd's own writings: the ideas that came to him while in that quiet "state of meditation" he often spoke of. Again, the words that came through in our conversations on the Friday nights, and in the early talks were different again, and were mainly inspired by our questions.

Even in his early public talks Syd paused often to ask for questions. He told us repeatedly that, often, he was hearing the answer for the first time, the same as we. But again, those Friday nights were our first experience with the teachings and, as I say, they were much more personal.

For example, let's say you are a woman with a husband and family, desperately searching for truth or the meaning of life. And you hang around Syd; you read his writings and books and listen to his tapes. You hang around with his other students and you listen to him every chance you get. Perhaps you attend groups, read all the current "in" books and consider yourself pretty enlightened. Then, one memorable moment, you are finally alone with him! You ask him all those questions about the esoteric meaning of life. In answer to your question about what should be next on your spiritual path, Syd responds, "Go home and clean your house!" Or, "Look after the kids and spend more time with them, instead of hanging around town all day shopping at the book store or the thrift store and sitting in the café with your friends."

Syd once told a big, strong, handsome fellow who had been a success at everything in life to spend more time just being quiet, to quit running around trying to teach truth that he didn't really understand, to quit smoking so much grass and playing his guitar and work more steadily to support his wife and kids, and then worry about his immortal soul.

It was hard sometimes. We loved him. We adored him. He was the gentlest person on the planet. No one could be as compassionate as Syd. If we all ganged up on someone who had strayed, erred, not gotten it, Syd could cut right through our discourse with a few words. Sternly, he might look at someone and say, "Okay, let's see what you'd do in that situation!"

None of us wanted the words that would impel us to make those scary, drastic changes in our lives, to leave behind our present sense of who we were. Yet, for those of us who did, in my case as in many others, I believe, we were desperate for the truth.

I, personally, had tried friends, relatives, then talks, meetings, then groups, then therapists and counsellors, then psychologists, then psychiatrists, then medication and shock therapy, and I had thought, "It didn't work!" But, as always with Syd, apparently I was wrong? Whining to Syd once over all these scary "crazy therapies" and my past experience, he stunned me once again.

"You were lucky!" he said.

"Sure," I thought! "Ever woke up from a shock treatment with a small stick lodged between your teeth so you don't bite your tongue off?!"

"If you had not had those experiences," Syd continued, "you would not have been ready for truth. You would not be here now. You would not be writing this book!"

"Gee, thanks," I thought. But of course, once again, he was right!

I believe the biggest hurdle on the path to self-realization is our fear of confronting our own demons. It is lovely to go and hear a Sydney Banks, an Eckhart Tolle, as long as they aren't telling you to get a job, take care of your health or change your kids diaper more often.

None of us wanted what we called a "workshop," yet I can see now just how privileged we were to have someone honest, fearless and brave enough to just cut through all the "games" we played; to get right down to the essence of things that were keeping us from growing. Syd would simply *not* play anyone's game. These "workshops," as we called them, could leave one in tears, angry, furious or scared. And countless people, at the juncture where they had gained a bit of access to Syd personally and thought they were on the way, just left.

The really deep learning came from those incredibly painful "workshops." We all took our turn. This was both the blessing and the curse of being so close to Syd, so close that we could be counted on as being his best friends. Yes, there was always that distance, that respect. All of us in the beginning, took these harsh words to heart. We listened, tried our best to make those changes, or I think we all knew we would not have the privilege of spending the countless, endless hours with Syd, before this quiet man became Sydney Banks, mentor and teacher to tens of thousands around the world. And we were first.

CHAPTER 14

THE LUCKY ONES

While none of us wanted those personal teachings, those "workshops", what we did want was only the "high" talk about consciousness, about the present moment, about what God really is—not the old white-haired gentleman sitting on a cloud that we could ask for favours, a new car or a new husband. We wanted it very high, very spiritual and very impersonal. Yet, it was these personal teachings that for some people, like myself, enabled one to just instantly *drop* a whole lifetime of conditioning from family, school, work and environment to get in touch with what Syd called "our True Self," another term he used constantly.

Yes, we loved it better sitting around the fire, or on the beach with Syd as he spoke quietly, waiting for those incomparable moments when he would kind of move off into another consciousness. Then, in those moments, a new and incredible world would be revealed. Some of these talks were, literally, beyond mind.

We did not know what he said, did not know what we "heard" but Bill and I would often drive home speechless—strange for me—after one of these occasions that were frequent in the early days. For the next few days life would be different, so different one could not really understand intellectually what had happened or what one had heard. The more one pondered this, the more it evaporated. Syd taught us to "just live," to "let it go, don't think about it, just live it."

In time this feeling would fade, and it could never be recaptured by thinking about it. Amazing learning experiences, life changing and life shattering, happened that way, and one might have an insight to quit their job, decide to actually commit to someone and get married, or start a business. The fall-out was startling.

"Energy" was one of Syd's favourite words, and he often talked about his experience and how he discovered that what we knew of as God was actually "the energy of all things." He would repeat this phrase over and over. He perceived everything as energy, and we learned a lot about it also. Not only was this universe just a thought, an energy field, but with our level of consciousness we turned that energy into either "positive" or "negative" energy.

Syd spoke about *levels of consciousness* constantly. I think I said before somewhere, that initially, I didn't know I even had one! If someone, a politician, a friend, a relative, did something that came up in the conversation, Syd might say:

"Well, that's just his level of consciousness!"

He might say, "Well, she needs help; she has a really low level of consciousness."

He taught us not to judge, for it turns out all of us have a level of consciousness, either higher (hopefully) or lower, but with each of us it fluctuates from day-to-day and goes up and down. No one is immune.

One Friday night, an event occurred that I will *never* forget! This was a time when perhaps only four or five of us were present. It was a fun and casual part of the evening, the way these amazing events always began. Suddenly, in answer to a question someone asked when Syd revealed he had taken karate—not a black belt, but close—Syd suddenly stood up from his chair, flipped over unto—well, I would say it was his hands but as I recall it was almost as though it were his fingertips—and then quickly moved across the room, over that carpet, standing straight up on his fingertips, flying across the room, body straight as an arrow, flying, flying across the room. I was speechless! I couldn't believe my eyes. We all sat in stunned silence! Then, Syd began to laugh. He knew he had us! We all laughed along with him, once again side-lined by this master of disguises, this master of secrets, our Master. The One who brought us to Truth!

* * *

First, it was the five couples, for perhaps six to eight months, then others appeared. Sometime they stayed and became lifelong students. Other times, someone would appear, usually someone we hippies had met, taken a liking to and felt they would make a nice addition to our little group. We would be stunned and shocked when Syd spoke and perhaps they would ask a really dumb question, then they might get testy over the answer, which obviously didn't coincide with their belief systems.

People got angry, felt hurt, stood up and walked out, argued back and forth trying to make a point, or all of the above. The rest of us would look on in horror and shock because we knew, here sits an enlightened man, and a hippie from Mayne Island is challenging him? I guess we all forgot our own early struggles.

After Syd's first talk at Central Hall, which a few locals

attended, several would come to his Friday night talks. A few became students for shorter or longer periods of time. Dave and Carol on Mayne had gathered a small group of followers around them, and within a year or so, more than a dozen students actually moved to Saltspring, including Michelle Grant, who took the photo that became the cover of *Island of Knowledge*, Tom Langois, and Chip and Jan Chipman who would work, travel and teach with Syd until his passing.

Friday nights now found around twenty people gathered to hear Syd, and word began to spread that there was indeed, an enlightened man on Saltspring Island. In his higher, quieter moments, when he had spoken for a while, and we had all quieted down, he would get around to talking about Self. Not the little small-self, but the bigger, universal Higher Self; the Universal Self.

Syd spoke often about "no thought" but it was not the no thought of, "I can't remember where I put the keys!" (or purse, or hammer, or child). I felt, on occasion, perhaps I experienced the "no thought" where thoughts just kind of stopped, stilled, and then knowledge came in instead of being thought up. I yearned for these moments, and they were too few and far between.

My very favourite, I think, was "going inside!" There evolved a very special sequence of events at our Friday nights. Mostly the evenings all followed the same pattern. We would gather in Syd and Barb's comfy living room. Most of the year; spring, fall and winter, it is cool enough by the sea to have the fireplace either glowing or roaring. Summer evenings, we might sit outside in the meadow. Once gathered and quiet, Syd would begin to speak. It was usually something new, for in those days, Syd didn't travel and spent most of his time at home just quietly writing and pondering.

We would sit, enraptured, following every word, for any word might be the one that we would *hear*. Syd would speak for perhaps ten or fifteen minutes, then ask if there were any questions. Normally, the questions would be serious questions from us seekers whose prime purpose in life had become knowing ourselves. Syd would answer our questions, usually in ways that completely blew our minds.

This would go on for a couple of hours, then came the part I lived for. We would have all settled down by now. Syd would have spoken, explained, explicated and expressed his deepest insights. A silence would descend. It is hard to describe this feeling. It was like being in church. As I recalled in an earlier chapter, I had spent much time in church — the serious, sacred consecrated atmosphere of the Catholic Church, complete with statues of the saints, the gold of the vestments, the smell of incense that wafted throughout the congregation, the incredible silence among perhaps hundreds of people as the tabernacle was opened, and the Host consecrated.

How to describe that this same feeling would be present in Syd's living room! Surely, it brought us to that feeling of "going inside" that Syd spoke of constantly, as what we were searching for. This feeling can only be described as "sacred," and I knew then I was indeed in the presence of someone who had touched a realm of existence that I could only guess at and humbly aspire to.

As with the others, these evenings changed my life. It was not until years, perhaps decades later, when I saw that my life had been radically changed by coming into the presence of this man — sitting with all faculties open and alive, quietly absorbing the secrets of the universe in a small white cottage near the sea, on a small island, a small universe.

Later, Syd would say that we five couples would never know how much we learned, that we didn't need to teach, for in our daily lives we were teaching with our minds, our thoughts, our hearts.

Jim Wallace:

We were together with Syd and Barb one evening at the home of a mutual friend. Someone marveled at how everything had grown from the five couples that once gathered together in the Banks' living room.

Syd looked at us for a moment.

"You were the lucky ones," he said. "You'll never stop changing!"

CHAPTER 15

BLISS NINNIES

As students moved to Saltspring from the other islands, the Big Island, and the Mainland, our small group grew. Most of us were in our twenties; some single, some, like Bill and I, living together, some married, and some with children. We were all new to island life and living in a small town.

Actually, it was a village. Everyone called Ganges "The Village." The Brits had named the Island, "Admiralty Island," which at some point had been renamed Salt Spring after the salt springs which trickled from the ground on an earthquake fault line just north of where we presently live.

In late 1973 when Bill, Gary and I bought our cottage in the woods, about 2000 people then lived on "The Rock," as locals called it. We weren't locals! You had to be here for ten years to be considered locals, then it grew to fifteen, and when we had been here fifteen years, it appeared to be twenty. Finally in 1994 we were eligible, but then the rules changed again. You had to have a family member born here to be a true "Local." Finally, when grand-son Owen appeared in 1999, we became locals!

I include this trivia to show what living on a very small island set in the middle of the Salish Sea, a three-hour ferry ride from Vancouver and a half-hour ferry ride from Vancouver Island, was like in 1974. The village was set on Ganges Harbour, a pretty little bay with docks and a Coast Guard station and dozens of sailboats and yachts that visited from the Vancouver and Seattle sailing clubs.

So, for a rural area, the Island was quite sophisticated. Elvis visited in those early days, when his manager was dating a local woman. Elvis never got off his extremely visible, very large yacht for fear of being mobbed. We were hysterical because we were Beatles and Rolling Stones fans, but Elvis, in his later years of wide belts and white flares? Sorry, not interested. His chances of being mobbed on the Island in 1974 were slim to none.

The economy was pretty much a few visitors; the hordes had not yet discovered Saltspring, and it was before such celebrities as Bill Gates, Barbara Streisand and Robin Williams came to escape the crowds in the idyllic hills, valleys and waterfront areas. A sleepy little retirement community with a few loggers, fishers and sheep-farmers left over from the old days, and a growing quotient of hippies.

Apparently, we were scary. We changed the village very quickly and visibly. On my first trip to the local "department store," an older gent in a suit followed a foot or so behind me, making sure I didn't shoplift, and he gently replaced everything just-so that I touched or looked at.

There were three restaurants on the Island, and when Bill and I first visited one we were asked by the waitress to leave. When we inquired why, we were told that it was because no jeans were allowed. I had on my nice long Indian bedspread, and Bill wore his usual jeans with the flowers, bolts of lightning and mushrooms I had embroidered. We began quietly to object, but she was adamant. She kept looking back over the counter to where the boss was standing silently.

Just then, a very straight-looking young man at a near-by table stood up. "But I'm wearing jeans," he said, "and you've served me!"

I can't remember the rest but the staff all became angry, shouted lots of reasons why we weren't allowed and ushered us, now really embarrassed, out. But, the only other café in town decided there were so many of us, they made hippies their clientele. We could nurse babies, push tables together in large groups and bring in our dogs if they sat quietly under the table.

But as the group of young people surrounding Sydney Banks grew, there emerged a growing hostility from the real locals. Most of them had never seen or heard Syd, and wouldn't have recognized him if they bumped into him on the street. But they recognized us! Soon, we heard that we had become known as "The Bliss Ninnies."

We were visible everywhere. Parent-school meetings. Wandering around the local park, which took up most of the downtown harbour area. Lounging on the grass, most of us drenched in Patchouli oil. Apparently, this scent was associated with hippies and thought to be the smell of marijuana, so we were always being asked to leave somewhere.

This was a strange sensation for me after my life as an executive assistant working in downtown Vancouver. A relative once chided us for visiting them "stoned-out-of-our-gourds," as they put it. Although I admit we some-times imbibed, that day we had just come off of a blissful three hour ferry ride complete with dancing dolphins and a few Orcas jumping in the Strait. But it was a memorable experience because, I realized, not only did I not look depressed, I was so genuinely happy that I looked stoned all the time. The relative, who shall remain nameless, declared it was my shiny, luminous eyes that gave me away.

And, of course, having met Sydney Banks and living happily ever after, we always had great big smiles on our faces. We were *so* happy! Yes! Bliss Ninnies! We were always gushy, as one new friend described us—always smiling.

Around this time Syd began to talk about "feelings," because many of his followers were not getting the message. We would memorize his words and could soon repeat his wonderful, mystical sayings. Those with a sharp intellect grasped the teachings quickly, and could quote Syd at will.

Once our small group continued to grow, from almost the beginning Syd had wanted us to tell people about what was happening to us, to our families. I can't remember who it was, Syd or one of us, who came up with the concept of "sharing!" Syd encouraged, even insisted, that we share, as he said it was the way for *us* to "get it!" He said it was by sharing our knowledge that it would become more real in our lives, and not just something to be talked about, or some arcane knowledge that we were studying.

Sheri:

> Soon after we met, Syd focused on the fact that I worked at the elementary school. He said it was important that I had such an audience to interact with. That if I could hear truth, it would affect the way I was with the children. He always told us, if your cup is full, no new knowledge can come in. You have to share to keep learning. For me, this was more

living it than speaking about it. As I felt more love, acceptance and understanding of others, I could provide the support they needed to find better answers within themselves. I could recognize the spark in them and help them see it, too.

Sharing would become perhaps the most important thing we did. Syd told us over and over that it was by sharing that we would learn, and we were learning more and more each day. To keep our good fortune, our renewed sense of well-being, our happier marriages (actually, almost none of us were legally married; it was 1974, after all), Syd taught us that, like him, we needed to pass along what we had learned. This concept would have a lot of repercussions—some wonderful, some beautiful, some rather unpleasant, and some downright scary.

Bill recalls how he would run into people and begin to give a lecture on the meaning of life in the local café or hardware store. Syd began to catch on that his idea of "sharing" the teachings was not working out the way he planned. He began to teach us that feelings were important and made a wonderful tape on the subject.

Once again, we all went off course. We believed by feelings he meant we must be happy all the time. Syd never taught that, never said we should be happy all the time. Syd was not happy all the time. He could be divinely joyous, mad at the stupidity of humanity, or at us personally. At other times, he was delighted, furious, puzzled sometimes about what to do next, where to take these teachings spawned by his incredible experience, how to share it, and so many other issues that we as normal, unawakened human beings did not have to experience.

As more students came into the group, a separation

seemed to develop between those who "got it" and those who didn't. Those who "got it" would be noticed by Syd. They might be invited out to dinner by him and others to share their experience. As time went on, it became of the utmost importance within our little group that one really *got it!* To show that we got it, we somehow thought it was necessary to be happy all the time. When someone truly *heard*, as Syd called it, one could see the visible change in their faces, manner and energy. So, unfortunately, it seemed necessary to be happy *all* of the time to prove one had indeed gotten it. Soon, ubiquitous smiles were everywhere. Thus, we became The Bliss Ninnies!

Sheri:

At times I would be uncomfortable around some of the people who considered themselves "disciples" that seemed to be trying too hard to be happy. It didn't ring true. However, when someone "heard" a truth it would be noticeable. They would shine! This happened to Don.

After I had attended a number of meetings with Syd, Don noticed a difference with me and decided he would come and see what it was all about. We were at a meeting in Vancouver when he had an experience. He didn't say anything afterwards, but his eyes and face glowed. He just looked beautiful, and people were gravitating to him, giving him hugs. I don't know what "clicked" with him that night, but our relationship just kept getting better.

However, I felt uncomfortable with some of the people that were his followers at the time, even though I was one myself, because they were "too gushy." It was like they were overly happy and it just rang as a bit fake. There were people who listened to Syd, got something from what he said and moved on with their lives because "the group" dynamic was not for them.

Syd recognized this from time to time when he noticed someone getting too carried away "manifesting cosmic energy" that was not real. I will always remember one of the group going on about a fly she had watched trapped on the window under her curtain. She said, "I loved the spiritual dance of this fly and realized it was the dance of the energy of all things!" As she carried on, Syd interrupted with a loud, "A FLY IS JUST SWAT!" In other words, it's just something to be swatted, not to be venerated – it's not the dance of life! She was embarrassed and shocked, but it was a good lesson for us all. Sometimes when he saw the group getting carried away, he had to be tough to bring us back to reality. We were not angels yet! Flies were just flies. Occasionally, we wanted to act more enlightened than we were, l.o.l.

Time passed, and as the separation between us and the other villagers grew, we became known as Sydney Bankers. We might be talking to someone in the super-market and hear, "Oh, You're one of those Sydney Bankers."

In those days we had a large hotel on Saltspring, the Harbour House, where boaters could moor and stay the night. It also housed the only public drinking establishment on the Island, with a restaurant, lounge and pub. We gathered there occasionally, although none of us were drinkers, because it was a large, open space with music where we could socialize. A large parking lot out back opened onto a hallway which led past the kitchen and into the pub. On one visit, I saw two interesting bits of graffiti on the hallway wall. One, I thought too funny! Someone had scrawled in giant letters "E$T" – the dollar sign summing up what we had heard about that popular, personal growth movement. The other piece of graffiti covered the wall for about six feet, written in giant letters. I can still see it in my mind's eye as though it were yesterday:

JESUS SAVES
SYDNEY BANKS

This no doubt resulted from the gossip making the rounds that Sydney Banks was making millions off innocent little groupies coming from the ends of the earth to hear his teachings. As in other communes, people brought their fortunes with them, while Sydney Banks relieved them of this bad karma to help save their souls.

Nothing could be further than the truth. Syd would not accept a penny for his help or teachings. We all offered to give and share what we had, but Syd would not accept money from us. One thing we could do, however, was help around the Banks' home to compensate for the countless hundreds of hours a month Syd spent helping the rest of us. We began to gather at the Banks' home regularly and have work bees.

We lasses baked goodies and snacks and cooked the lunches, while the men mowed the lawn, chopped wood, and helped with renovations on the small cottage. It was the least we could do, as the Banks' were living on the proceeds of the house they had sold in Nanaimo before coming to live with Mary in her small cottage.

As the group began to grow Syd travelled with this entourage to Mayne Island, Courtenay, Vancouver Island locations, with several visits to The Big Smoke, as we disparagingly called Vancouver. We often visited Nanaimo to meet Syd's old co-workers and friends. Ken and Elsie Spittle would later move to Saltspring, along with Larry and Sandy Clarkson. Both men worked at the pulp mill with Syd. Other friends soon joined them in moving to

Saltspring, among them Sandra Clapham, Richard and Marika Meyer, and Heather and Peter Braun.

As Syd began to travel more, with all of us Bliss Ninnies accompanying him, our sheer numbers encouraged others to come and listen. Many would then make the move to Saltspring Island. Events multiplied in a way that seemed wonderful and exciting, and we believed this growing phenomena meant we were very highly evolved and very successful at helping to share Syd's dynamic and soulful teachings.

CHAPTER 16

ISLAND OF KNOWLEDGE

As the first year and season drew to a close we began to look forward to Christmas. Not surprisingly, this year the holidays would not be like those previous. There were no rounds of boisterous parties, over-indulging with food, drink, or whatever. True to our new-found quieter, more insightful life, things became more simple, more real.

A chapter in *Island of Knowledge* would be devoted to this time, and Syd's words about Christmas would change our perception of this event for all time. I quote from that lovely time Syd's own words: "It isn't the giving or receiving of presents that is important. It is the giving of love and understanding that matters."

Best Christmas ever!

The Becks and the Wallaces had disappeared to visit family, and Bill, Gary and I left for Mission, B.C. to spend the holiday with Bill's family — his parents, five sisters and their husbands and kids. Although it was a warm and familiar scene with gifts galore, and we loved it, their exuberance stood in sharp contrast to the quiet space we had spent with the Banks' leading up to Christmas day.

Yet, with those quiet evenings spent on the Island in the last week before Christmas came a new experience. A picture in *Island of Knowledge*, taken by Carol, shows Syd and Barb, their Nanaimo friends Ken and Elsie Spittle, Bill and I, and Dave Simpson sitting together on that now famous carpet after a fondue dinner party. Only days before Christmas I had finished the manuscript for *Island of Knowledge*. What an exciting time! We were all excited about seeing the book in print, but Syd felt it was not happening fast enough.

Syd appeared one day, as I was finalizing the last proof of the book and said it couldn't wait. He and Barb, along with Dave and Carol, had thought up titles for all the chapters. I had been working so diligently on this project I was a little taken aback. In three or four days I would have the manuscript complete. But I had to admit that their titles brought the chapters to life and made the small book feel somehow complete.

New Year's Eve ushered in 1975, which would be one of the most exciting times of my entire life. I couldn't believe the book had actually been written, finished, and would soon be copyrighted and printed. Students of Yogi Bhajan in Vancouver, who ran the 3HO Foundation, agreed to publish the book. They edited and designed the book for us, then we paid $1500.00 to have the book printed. With our limited budget, and Bill's small income as a local handyman, we had to get a loan to print the book, but we would sooner have seen it in print than purchase a new car. Off to press it went, and then began an entire year of travelling, telling our story, and selling books.

I am not sure of the exact dates of where we went, but we spent that whole year on the road. We visited Mayne Island, where Dave and Carol lived and had gathered a small group of students around them. We went to the Nanaimo area, where Syd and Barb had lived and worked for many years. We visited various locations on Vancouver Island, including Courtenay. We made many, many visits to Victoria, where a group also formed. Ultimately we progressed to Vancouver, and by then, we were a growing phenomenon.

This had happened gradually. As we grew too large for Syd's living room, we first ventured a mile or two just down the country road to Central Hall. Built a century ago as an agricultural hall during pioneer days, the hall later became our theatre, and remains so to this day. It was easy to rent, and free to all community groups. We gathered our cushions and kids and went to Central Hall. I remember little about that day, but photos I took show cushions and carpets covering the floor, and a group of long-hairs sitting around discussing the nature of life. Even though we advertised a bit, we didn't get a huge reception, but at least we were now out in public. My records show this was May 6, 1975.

In June, Syd put on his white "guru" outfit, and we all headed for Courtenay, B.C. Pictures from that era and in *Island of Knowledge* show Syd dressed this way, and that is a story in itself. The 3HO Foundation in Vancouver had sent over the first of their members to teach on Saltspring Island; the young man from whom I learned Kundalini Yoga just before I met Syd. Now they were editing and designing *Island of Knowledge* and preparing it for the printing process. Bill and I got to know several of them, and some of us had journeyed over to one of their meetings. Syd had also spoken there one night, and although we missed this for some reason, I well recall his comments when he returned. After he spoke, someone had mentioned that Syd did not "look" like a guru! Indeed, he didn't. Mostly, he wore jeans and a nice shirt, often plaid, like most of us Canucks. Plaid shirts? So, this isn't how people wanted their "guru" to look?

Syd became a Master at reinventing himself to whatever the moment required, whatever he believed would help his message best get out at the time. You want a guru? Okay, I'll give you a guru. Remember, most if not all of his students at that time were spiritual seekers and hippie-types. Our contemporaries, like the Beatles, were going to India, travelling around Nepal and Tibet looking for enlightened Masters, and so on. Ram Dass, with his PhD in Psychology or whatever, wore white cotton.

It so happens I was an excellent seamstress; I had specialized in cooking and sewing in Home Ec in high school. By this time I was making all the curtains and bed-spreads for our home, sewing all my own clothes, making shirts for Gary and Bill, including the jeans that Bill wore and that I became locally famous for. These jeans had lightning bolts made out of bright yellow scraps of fabric I hunted out at the local thrift. There were red hearts, trees, fungi, flowers and so on. As we were among the early hippies on the Island, sometimes regular folks kind of looked stunned when we appeared with my floor length tie-dye skirts, embroidered tops, and Bill's famous jeans.

So I offered to make an outfit for Syd, one suitable for formal talks, tasteful and attractive. I travelled to Vancouver and visited the area's top fabric shop. I bought yards and yards of the finest, softest, most expensive white cotton available. I designed the pattern myself, for I had learned to sew from patterns, and learned this skill in Home Economics. I also purchased patterns with embroidery on them. I purchased skeins and skeins of embroidery thread in all colours and began my project. I spent all my spare time, and we had lots of that, but still it took about two weeks to complete the outfit.

I have to admit, the day I took the finished product over to Syd's and he disappeared into the bedroom to try them on, I held my breath. When he reappeared, Barb, Bill and I were stunned. After our stunned silence, we burst out laughing and clapping. He looked *so* handsome, so perfect! We had found our spiritual guru! Not only did he speak like one, act like one, but now he also looked like one. There are a lot of pictures of Syd in this outfit, with its flared pants, flared cuffs with no collar—the kind of Nehru look popular at the time.

When we visited Courtenay on June 21, 1975, Syd wore the outfit, and no one ever commented or seemed to find it strange. It just seemed so perfect for the times, and it was. Among the mostly young people like us who were attracted to his talks, this was the way a spiritual guide should and must look.

In Courtenay, a crowd of twenty or thirty people appeared. It was a lovely talk. There was no challenging Syd, no eye-ball rolling. The dozen or so of us that accompanied him also helped, I believe, to give him credibility. People later said they were attracted by how happy and calm Syd and Barb were, and how happy and exuberant all his students were.

Mayne Island came next, in July of that year. Carol and Dave Simpson, Barb's brother, had shared their experiences and the magic in their lives with their friends and neighbours on Mayne Island. They lived on a property near the lighthouse on a point of land jutting out to sea. It was magic. After the talk we gathered at the hall with the locals for a Virginia reel. I had never attended such a thing; only seen the like in old Westerns, perhaps. Bill and I loved to dance and have several trophies to prove it. We never had so much fun.

However, one thing occurred that disturbed me deeply. Scores of people attended, probably because only once or twice a year a speaker of some kind might come to the Island. Those of us who were the early students met Syd, heard him speak for four or twelve minutes, and then became students for life. We were always slightly puzzled, I think, when we brought friends to the Friday night gatherings, and they asked what we thought were crazy questions or began to challenge Syd's words, or talked about what Ram Dass or Carlos Castaneda or Yogi Bhajan had said. This night, at the end of Syd's talk, when he asked if there were any questions, which he invariably did, a young man stood up, and in quite a nasty, challenging way, put Syd down, inferring that Syd knew nothing, had no credentials and was talking nonsense. I was stunned. How could anyone hear his message, sit when Syd was at his highest moments in that incredible silence that always ensued when he spoke, and react in this manner?

I was a neophyte at the time, I guess, because we would experience this time and again as Syd, with us following, set out into the wider world to spread the teachings. Once the book came out, and there were tapes to sell, just like at rock concerts, I believe Syd gained more and more credibility. His name became known all over the NorthWest, and I think if people thought he was a charlatan they just didn't come. So this kind of event changed over time, although there always were and probably always will be the nay-sayers around. But the first time I experienced this, my small world kind of spun. I can't remember the exact first experience where this happened — whether it was someone who had come to our early group, friends of ours or the Becks or the Wallaces — but the first time I heard someone challenge Syd's words instead of listening quietly at his feet, so to speak, I had been quite taken aback.

Syd, as usual, explained everything to us. It was all about levels of consciousness, he said. Some people — and he did not judge them — are just not ready for *Truth*.

"But," he always continued, "You can't water it down!" I would hear these words again and again. Syd would not ever change his words or his teachings to make them more palatable or explainable to those who challenged him or asked him to make things more simple so that they could better understand.

With the publication of *Island of Knowledge*, I believe Syd and his teachings gained a huge amount of credibility, and suddenly many of Syd and Barb's friends, acquaintances, and co-workers from Nanaimo began to visit Saltspring, and Syd began to spend more time travelling to visit those eager now to hear his message.

Syd in his white outfit, made by Linda

CHAPTER 17

SCIENCE OF MIND

Syd was fascinated with the books that appeared in his life along with his students. The students came from every walk of life, and often from various other spiritual disciplines they had been involved with, and they brought books with them.

Carlos Castaneda was a favourite of Bill and me. We read him voraciously. We shared those books with Syd and discussed them at length. I especially loved *Separate Realities*, for it tied in so wonderfully with Syd's teachings, and we spent many, many nights talking about the separate realities we all lived in.

Jim Wallace:

Syd really enjoyed Separate Realities, *and even contended that the Don Juan character was Castaneda himself!*

As with all the beliefs and ideas we had about the spiritual life and life in general, Syd explained *Separate Realities* in a way that Don Juan never managed to convey. We were so deep into this concept that finally we taped one of Syd's talks in his living room about it. Bill's time with the rock and roll band came in handy, and he became Syd's first tape man.

Later, new students involved with the *Infinite Way* would bring some of Joel Goldsmith's books around, and I remember someone gave me Joel's, *The Art of Meditation*, which was nothing like any meditation we were doing in the '70s! Another student had spent some time in a monastery in the States, and brought a book we'd never heard of: *The Impersonal Life* by Joseph Benner, penned in the early 20th Century. Many of us, including Syd, bought and read it over and over while we encouraged Syd to talk about its concepts, which we loved, but of course, did not understand.

Many people say that Syd read no or very few books. This is understandable because Syd, himself, wanted to be sure that people knew his enlightenment experience did not come from books but from his own direct experience, which it did. So Syd may have overcautiously understated his reading habits, which others then picked up on.

The wonderful and magical thing about all this was Syd could take any concept, no matter how esoteric or unfathomable, and explain it fully in his own words. He brought all those books to life for us, and it was really gratifying to me that he did not put down or criticize in any way the books we were reading in our search.

One day when Syd appeared to work on our second book, he brought along a book he had just found at the landfill. Syd was beside himself. I took one look at the book, and thought, "Uh, oh! Syd's lost it!" The cover was missing. Probably the first ten or twelve pages and the last part of the book with the appendix were curled up shreds of paper. The hundreds of pages (this was a very, very thick book) were all curled up and lined and underlined with pencil. It struck me that someone had spent forty years reading this book every day, trying again and again to understand it. That they had probably passed away, and their heirs would have sent what was left of the book to the trash.

Jim Wallace:

One stormy night we huddled around our fire while the wind howled outside, when we heard Syd's voice calling to see if we were home. He burst into the tepee with his young daughter Susan, and appeared very excited.

"This is unbelievable!" he said. "I've found the book I've been looking for all my life!" He told us how he and Sue had taken a load of trash to the local landfill, when he noticed a book lying open in the mud at his feet.

"I picked it up," he continued, "and there was the secret of life before my very eyes!"

He handed it to Judy and showed her how he had marked pages for us to read.

"There is pure truth on every page!"

The book had no cover, but we later found it was The Science of Mind, *by Ernest Holmes, written almost a century earlier as a roadmap for living a spiritual life.*

I quickly went to our local bookshops to see if I could find it. Even then, in the early '70s, Saltspring had three or five bookshops for a population of around 2000. I have heard it said that Saltspring is the "home of the intelligencia in Canada." The bookshops didn't have it. They checked to see who might, and none of their suppliers had access to it. Finally, after weeks of persistent pressure and diligent searching, someone found it could be ordered from Britain. The price of course was prohibitive, probably several days wages at the time. I ordered it regardless, and proudly showed it to Syd.

After devouring its pages, almost none of which I understood, I decided to lend it to Syd. It would be more than three decades later when I received it back.

So, did Syd "copy" things he read or became inspired by? Not at all. Any spiritual book I have ever read or looked at, including the Bible, are full of quotes, ideas and concepts from other lands, eras and writers. Our truly transformative experience in reading any of the books circulating at that time from students on the path came when Syd read them over, and in a way only he could do, totally translated those ideas and concepts into language we could understand.

With Syd, Mind, Consciousness and Thought came alive and held real meaning for us, much deeper than we could extract from the more ponderous writings of Ernest Holmes from the distant past.

CHAPTER 18

GATHERING OF THE WAYS

With publication of *Island of Knowledge* in late spring of 1975, my life had once again changed completely! Now, Bill and I were travelling constantly to a round of bookshops who were happy to carry *Island of Knowledge* and push it as a local book and local author. Many had now heard of Sydney Banks, so bookshops in Courtenay, Nanaimo, Victoria and Vancouver would help us to sell almost 2000 copies of the book in the next year or two.

The local bookshop, whose owner I knew, agreed to have a book-signing. It was advertised and attended by quite a few islanders, and lots of copies of the book sold. Suddenly I was a local celebrity, among the other fifty or so local published authors.[4]

Syd encouraged and inspired us constantly and convinced me that someday, as he became known worldwide, I would be a world-famous author and Bill and I would make our living selling the book and others that would come after. It certainly seemed something big was happening.

---

[4] However, over 40 years later, most people on the Island have now never heard of Sydney Banks, and I never did become world famous or even Island famous, and as the years passed, *Island of Knowledge* passed into ancient history, with an occasional copy showing up at used book sales. Sydney Banks will likely become increasingly famous, as his teachings continue to spread even after his death. *Island of Knowledge* was republished in 2015 by CCB Publishing, British Columbia.

At each talk Syd gave, the whole group of serious students—which now had grown to about fifty or sixty—would accompany him, and he would talk about the book and have me give a short talk about my experiences, and we would prominently display the book. During the break, while people mingled and had a chance to speak with Syd personally, Bill and I would sell books.

We felt like Rock Stars, and we dressed the part. I made Bill a fancy shirt or two, and I think he blushes now when we look at our old photo albums. I created long tie-dyed skirts for myself that swept the floor, and embroidered everything I wore. With Syd in his outfit, Bill and I in our post-Woodstock fashions, and most of our fellow students dressed in a similar way, we must have made quite a show.

Although I never became a formal teacher and didn't want to, Syd suggested our way of sharing was with the book. So as we gained experience at these talks Syd began to send us out on our own to share our experiences and spread word of the amazing happenings on the Island by sharing the book. I remember a succession of church basements, where a table could be spread out and we would stand and give a talk, sometimes with others like Dave and Carol, whom Syd would ask to accompany us. I also recall speaking in school gyms, where perhaps a dozen or so people would look lost in such a large location.

As word spread it became easier and easier to attract people to our talks, and crowds at Syd's talks grew exponentially. It was happening! A large bookshop in Duncan, B.C. carried the book and sold lots of copies, as this was a phenomenon happening right in the area. Then, we visited Atman Books, the center of the spiritual world in Victoria, B.C.

They loved the book! Bill and I were asked to come and make a small presentation, and they featured and advertised the book. Thus, a large group of people from Victoria became students and followers. By the time we visited Vancouver, and the famous Banyan Books, who sold not dozens, but hundreds of copies, Sydney Banks had become a force to be recognized in the West Coast spiritual scene.

Now, everywhere we went, excitement reigned. Lots of people flocked about, wanting to meet Syd, wanting to hear him speak, wanting to see what all the talk was about. It became more and more difficult to spend time with Syd, and for many, they were only able to see or speak with him at public events. Luckily, we were always communicating and working together over distributing the book—at this time the only way the message was spreading.

However, my sudden celebrity was both a blessing and a curse. On one hand, Bill and I were invited out for dinner almost every night. We became *so* popular—real celebrities in our circle of fellow students. However, travelling around and sometimes "pushing" the book went against my quiet nature.

I loved the quiet times working with Syd at the kitchen table with no one else around, perhaps Barb bringing tea occasionally. Or perhaps we would sit in the meadow with the waves always within earshot, and the magic vista of the strait and other small islands. But, pressure mounted to sell the book as more people arrived, as interest in Syd's teachings grew and as we travelled to new locations. I would have rather stayed home to write books.

Then, another milestone occurred when Sydney Banks was invited to The Gathering of the Ways! We made it. Big time!

Gathering of the Ways took place at Jericho Beach in Vancouver on August 9, 1975. Jericho Beach was the scene of one of British Columbia's first organized protests, which in later years our province would become famous or infamous for our leading-edge environmentalism and activism. To this day thousands gather here for the big music festival, and it lies at the end of 4th Avenue, which in the late '60s and early '70s became the home of Canada's first hippie shops and cafes. One could walk down 4th, as we called it, and have American draft dodgers offer a snort of hashish or an ounce of marijuana, which up to that time was rarely seen. 4th Avenue was also the place for silly little Saltspring hippies to purchase the latest fashions that hippies should be wearing, and see long hair and skirts on gals, Nehru shirts on guys, all of whom had beards and long hair.

I don't remember whether Sydney Banks was the keynote speaker or not, but we became an instant hit. Syd's talk was mind-blowing, and we were now on the spiritual map in Vancouver. My photo album shows Sydney Banks sitting on a stage festooned with rainbow flags.[5] With him are Chip Chipman on guitar and another couple of guys with vast amounts of hair in the background. Another photo shows Barb Banks and the elderly Mary Simpson wearing long skirts also and joining in the fun. I am in my au courant hippie outfit, holding a large bouquet of flowers. At an appropriate moment I ascended the stage and presented the flowers to Syd. I remember Sufi dancing

---

[5] In those days, the rainbow was not a LGBTQ symbol, but meant the family of hippiedom.

on stage that day, which led me to Rumi and his soulful poetry.

A ritual had evolved in our group, beginning, I would think, with Jim Wallace who played guitar beautifully. Also, Jim Beck played guitar, and Bill the harmonica, although badly. I bought a tambourine in Gastown, which had become the name of the 4th Avenue area where the New Age hippies gathered. Someone had bongos, and we began early on to add music to the Friday nights at Syd and Barb's. Syd loved the music. Each evening would end with a few tunes, and we would all stand up and sway, sing, bang bongos, shake tambourines and afterwards, hug each other. It was not only a silly hippie ritual, but after two or three hours listening to Syd, we were all in a kind of state of ecstasy. It is now hard to describe those long-ago days and the feeling we had. But we all loved each other unconditionally then, and were family — although a family with no hang-ups, issues to resolve or bad feelings.

At our first meeting at Central Hall, then Courtenay, the guys played their guitars at the end of the meeting. Now, it became de rigueur, and each meeting concluded with a hippie rock concert. While the guys played we girls clapped, or in my case banged my tambourine. (I was also Bob Dylan's greatest fan.) Soon we encouraged everyone to clap along with us, and most people who attended these gatherings left, like us, in a happy, elevated mood. Syd did not participate but sat glowing and smiling at the love, happiness and music surrounding him. Even though he would never see himself as such, I think he was always a closet hippie, myself.

At The Gathering of the Ways we took our performance to a new level. With Syd's new followers from

Courtenay, Nanaimo and Mayne Island we numbered about thirty, but The Gathering was our largest audience ever and our enthusiasm led a couple of hundred people to clap, sing, and smile along with us. We were definitely the big attraction and now we had rock star status among a certain segment of the general population.

The next talk was Beaver Point Hall on Saltspring, Syd's first large, advertised, public talk on Saltspring. The following events again shocked me, but in hindsight Beaver Point was just the catalyst for something that had been growing.

Linda at Gathering of the Ways

Syd at Gathering of the Ways

CHAPTER 19

BEAVER POINT

Looking back after three or four decades, things begin to fade, memories blend events together that may have happened years apart. Luckily, I have always kept a photo journal of my life. No, not a prize-winning photographer; but I've always had a cheap little point and click at my disposal and captured just about everything. Photos in our family album from that time capture some important dates, and as memory serves, or doesn't, the Beaver Point talk took place on August 23, 1975.

A few days prior to this seminal event, our local newspaper, the *Gulf Islands Driftwood* published an article. We locals often referred to the paper as the "Deadwood" when it was boring and only contained local politics, which at that time we were not remotely interested in. But we *loved* the August 20th issue, with its article entitled "Sidney Banks...Mystic or Prophet or Man of Wisdom?"

Speaking recently with the editor, it appears the article was "contributed" by a Brenda Anderson, not written by a usual staff member or reporter. I do not personally remember such a person working for the *Driftwood*, and it seems no one else remembers her either. Also, Brenda was not part of our "group" or a student of Syd's, as far as I can remember. Another mystery to be solved.

The article contains several inaccuracies, including the idea that two hundred people every day visited Syd and Barb at home. In those days the Island's entire population was around two thousand, and there were not enough ferries or B&Bs or resorts to handle this kind of traffic. Although in later years, many visitors from all over came to check things out, I could not even imagine over fifty people, which was about the largest number of people who came years later to organized meetings we conducted.

Sidney Banks...Mystic or Prophet or Man of Wisdom?[6]

By Brenda Anderson

Call him a mystic: call him a prophet: Sydney Banks is, perhaps, each of these, but this quietly-spoken Salt Spring Islander is a leader of men and women over a wide area.

Sydney Banks is gaining recognition in all of the West Coast as something of an oracle. People flock to his door, not to hear his answer to their problems, but to have him lead them to their own answer.

Unknown a few months ago, he is, today, the subject of tales, books and reports, while his time is now taken up with travelling and speaking.

Call him what you will...you cannot refuse to recognize that Sydney Banks has something going for him. But there is nobody yet to define just what that is.

"Nature is simply taking care of herself." More people are becoming aware; good things are coming together. Sydney Banks is providing a strong motivating force in that direction.

This gentle man offers simple truths. His manner of speaking seems to open doors. He doesn't profess to hold the keys,

---

[6] *Gulf Islands Driftwood*, August 20, 1975

the keys are in your own hands. In his unassuming way, he is sharing the self-realization that came to him two years ago.

Sydney Banks is a prophet of modern times. He brings about positive responses. A leader on a pedestal, he is not: and he has no 'followers' as such. The people he has reached, merely share the love and truths he conveys.

Sydney Banks is a 44 year old family man. His wife, Barbara, and their children live here on Salt Spring Island. Syd is a former welder. He had no formal education beyond age fourteen. He was not an avid reader of books; he was on no conscious search for the 'secrets of life.' There is no logical explanation for the enlightenment that came to him, nor is there a need for one. His life has simply reflected the change. People close to him picked up the glow, and it has been spreading ever since.

Speaking with a soft Scottish burr in his voice, Sydney Banks has a gift for clarity. His wisdom puts into words many unexplained realities of life. The knowledge he has found, with the gift of communication, unclouds obvious truths. Syd offers no trips, no confusing complexities. He brings people to a realization. Nothing is forced. There is no preaching. When he speaks, he seems to hold a mirror before you. Through his guiding words, he can express truths basic to being. He brings to acknowledgement, things so deep-rooted we have become unaware of them. He puts human games into a new light, and possesses the power of understanding and perception that helps people to truly see themselves.

Throughout the ages, humanity has had enlightened men in their midst. Sydney Banks does not claim to have new concepts. He only speaks the truth he knows. On occasion, something he says will be pointed out as a quote from a wise man of bygone times. Syd, not ever having seen the book, merely shrugs his shoulders, saying "He knew, also."

Sydney Banks' recognition is snowballing. He produces a chain-like-reaction. It is not uncommon for 200 people to pass through the Banks' home within three days. His time is becoming more and more in demand. He has been travelling and speaking on Vancouver Island, the outer islands, and on the mainland.

People respond with energy.

They ask for tapes, writings, whatever they can obtain. The gatherings have grown so large a normal-sized home is not adequate. Halls must be rented. Syd has no extra time for his welding profession. Posters have been printed to inform people so that they may share. There are books to be published.

There is one coming in the near future. Incidentally, written by a young woman from Salt Spring about the experiences shared through Sydney Banks.

Thus, it has become necessary to set up a Foundation. This non-profit institution will provide a means, establish a base, and cope with legal technicalities.

Sydney Banks is not a spectacular man: he is simply a wise man. A man with the gift of being able to share, teach, and spread this wisdom. His awareness is basic to all of us. He has the insight to be able to make others aware. He appeals to the "inner-most."

When the Maharishi visited here a few years back, he made the statement that Salt Spring Island could become the spiritual center of the world. That could well be...we have Sydney Banks.

This article had an amazing effect on our little group.

It created a communal feeling of euphoria, which only added to the palpable excitement we felt over our first *big* public gathering on Saltspring. During the previous summer, we had gained a lot of experience doing our thing at Courtenay, Mayne Island, and mostly Gathering of the Ways. Everywhere, everyone we knew or met only talked about one thing: Beaver Point.

We also printed an advertisement in the August 20th *Driftwood*, under "Coming Events."

A MIRACLE IS OCCURRING on Salt Spring Island! An enlightened man has appeared on the Island and is sharing his wisdom with all who seek the freedom of true peace, tranquility, love and understanding in their lives. An enlightened man is one who has directly realized or experienced the truth about all mankind: that we are each a conscious center in an infinite sea of energy we call the universe or God: that our true nature is God. Sydney Banks is an enlightened man. His teachings are transforming the lives of all who hear him. Marriages long full of frustration and boredom have miraculously turned into intensely joyful relationships. Children have changed from noisy irritating hindrances to calm, beautiful wise wee people full of laughter, joy and health. Such complaints as migraine headaches, allergies, back problems, hypertension and eyestrain have disappeared. All of us have become more beautiful, healthier, energetic and more loving. Sydney Banks lives on Salt Spring Island. He is here and available now to show all of us the way to experience truth directly. His words have the power to turn the lives of all who hear him into a literal paradise! Everyone has the opportunity to hear this beautiful man and share in the music and joy of his wisdom this Saturday, August 23rd at Beaver Point Hall at 7 pm.

I made myself a new outfit, a flared, embroidered

cotton blouse, and an amazing work-of-art long skirt, cut on the bias so it whirled and flared as I "willowed."[7] I brought my tambourine, of course; the only instrument I could play. Marty Lipsky played his dulcimer, Jim Wallace and Chip Chipman their guitars, with most of the guys on bongos. It was to be our biggest gathering yet.

With our advertisement, and with the *Driftwood* article so fresh in everyone's mind, the evening became the most talked-about event on the Island for months, perhaps years. We were all so proud to be part of this seminal event, and knew it would put Syd's name out there in front for all the public to see, not just the cluster of mostly hippies that usually surrounded him. Syd, too, was excited. This would introduce *truth* to the Island, and touch all those who did not yet know an enlightened man stood in their midst.

Besides the Maharishi saying "This will someday be the spiritual capital of the world," we also had the first Tibetan Buddhist monastery in North America on Mt. Tuam, and the Salt Spring Centre had been established by a group of people who were students of Baba Hari Dass, who did not speak but had a vow of silence. In later years, world teacher Eckhart Tolle would make the island his home. But now there was Sydney Banks.

* * *

---

[7] Willowing: the kind of "dancing" we did in those days. The men usually stood by, clapping and shuffling about. Ladies stood fairly still, swaying and moving their upper bodies around while arms were waved sensually in the air. We did this for hours.

Beaver Point was the "Turning Point." At the time, I felt very "high" during the entire gathering—not on drugs, just the euphoria of Syd and our group hitting the big-time on the Island. As our group grew, mutterings of dissent could be heard by the locals, who understandably perhaps were scared by our arrival on a very small island, with a very small population of loggers, farmers and a few old retired teachers and engineers from the big city who had small seaside cottages on the Island.

Saltspring was rumoured to be the first bastion of hippiedom in Canada. Here the first "long hairs" went back to the land. Many were draft dodgers from the U.S. in opposition to the Vietnam War. They brought with them something we had never heard of, marijuana, and there was no better place to grow it than the Island, with its vast areas of wilderness, open meadows amidst the old growth cedar and firs, old pasturage from abandoned homesteads of early pioneers, and mild Mediterranean climate.

The first hippie to arrive with long hair and a beard was rumoured to have visited one of the three local restaurants, where the good-ole-boys grabbed him and cut off his ponytail. When waves of us began to arrive, and then what they believed to be a cult leader appeared, I think a kind of panic set in among some people. These were the days of hippie communes in the U.S., with gurus who had seventeen Rolls Royces, dozens of courtesans, and money that his followers begged, borrowed and stole.

Around this time, we were often accused of being a cult. Well, I suppose we could have been considered "an alternative kind of sect not recognized as a church who followed the teachings of a charismatic leader." But Syd kept saying, "Don't follow me; the answer lies within each and every one of you." He certainly didn't get rich off his students from his teachings. Yet, despite Syd's efforts to the contrary, many people did follow him, and among them it could be said that a certain group ethos had begun to develop.

Syd gave an incredible talk at Beaver Point.

Sheri:

> In August of 1975 we had a meeting at Beaver Point Hall, and it was a large crowd by then. There was a yoga guy with long, flowing hair and white robes and a very spiritual aura about him, and soft spoken. He began to argue with Syd about what Syd was saying and interrupting him when he was speaking.

> It seemed a shame that this guy was so enlightened, in a way, but he was not open to hearing anything more, and you could see his defenses were up. He was determined to hold onto his belief and his biggest belief was in meditation. That meditation was the road to enlightenment. I remember Syd saying, "You can't find enlightenment by sitting and staring at your belly-button!" I think he was in a moment of exasperation by this time.

The event would be the last of its kind. An incredibly negative article appeared in the *Driftwood* the next week, written and submitted by an anonymous "observer."

Jim Wallace at Beaver Point

CHAPTER 20

NO MORE WILLOWING

The first hint of the wave of destruction that would follow happened the morning after.

Many of us had gathered earlier on Saturday afternoon before the talk to do our usual decorations at the Hall. We didn't take the stacked chairs out of the next room but spread as many cushions as we could gather, and we had a lot of them. Bill and I had sold the nice comfortable sofa and chairs I'd had in my Vancouver home, and would now sit or lie on said cushions while playing chess, drinking herbal tea out of small pottery cups I had made myself, and listening to "Stairway to Heaven" by the Led Zeppelin. The next morning after Syd's beautiful talk, Sunday, we were all supposed to arrive early, according to arrangements made with the Hall, clean up the Hall, put everything away and sweep the floor.

At the appointed time, 10:00 a.m., Bill and I arrived to find the hall empty. Oh well, so, we were first. It was hard getting up that morning. I felt like I had a hangover, although I hadn't drank for about ten years. I realized I had been incredibly hyper dressing for the talk, setting up the Hall, and although generally I was pretty speedy and hyper I had surpassed even my usual manic energy the night before, willowing, chatting and sharing. I felt "bummed out," which was one of Syd's favourite descriptions of people who experienced a low level of consciousness.

Shortly after, Syd and Barb arrived. They looked kind of bummed out as well, like a drop after a big high. We waited and quietly chatted. Syd became increasingly visibly frustrated as no one else appeared. Eventually, a couple of others showed up, but it was kind of a sad and mournful ending to the big event. The vast Hall, or so it seemed then, had to be swept up, and it was my duty to collect and wash all the coffee cups and clean up the kitchen where we had served coffee and cookies.

Syd definitely was "not impressed," as we used to say when he was not happy over something someone had done—hopefully not me. We all left in a kind of funk. We didn't hear from Syd or anyone in the next few days.

Then on Wednesday, the following letter to the editor appeared in the *Driftwood*:

LOOKING FOR ANOTHER MIRACLE*

After reading the two-page spread in the last week's Driftwood, "Sidney Banks – Mystic or Prophet or Man of Wisdom?" I felt that if even half of the gushing superlatives were true, I'd like to hear him. So my wife and I went to Beaver Point Hall last Saturday at the advertised time of 7 p.m. We then learned that (a) it was to start at 7:30 p.m. – not 7 p.m. and (b) there was an admission charge of $1.50 each.

Having paid $3 we entered the hall – largely occupied by bearded young long-hairs and their female companions. The air was heavy with the sweetish smell of marijuana, and we had to sit on tiny cushions on the floor. We were then bombarded by a collection of shaggy people, and long-skirted females, who banged on bongo drums and guitars while they moaned and chanted and swayed and stomped. This cacophony kept up until 7:45 p.m. – when some courageous *male yelled "We came to hear Banks!"*

Sidney (or Sydney) Banks was then introduced by "Jimmy" who said his life and wife were now beautiful, since talking to Banks.

Banks sat on the stage, surrounded by candles, and for an hour kept saying over and over, "Life can be beautiful. It is so simple. You must believe, and start living NOW. The past is gone forever, and the future is just a bunch of to-morrows."

This was dandy; but first, the faint half-whisper half-monotone he used made much of what he tried to say quite inaudible. Secondly, his Scotch accent didn't seem to clarify his diction. (He pronounced 'person' as 'pare-sun', etc.)

On leaving, I felt like the chap who'd read the glowing ad about a new book. After sending for, and reading the book, he wrote to the publisher, saying "I wish the man who wrote the ad had written the book."

Maybe I'm being too harsh and critical. If Sydney Banks could convert even the hundred or more hippie-types who attended the aforementioned gathering, into industrious, self-supporting, clean-living citizens: I'll also say, "A miracle is occurring on Salt Spring Island."

Signed: Observer

Whoa! Syd had an idea of who had written the article, and was more furious than I had ever seen him—not only at the anonymous "observer" but at all the rest of us. Syd and Barb had always been pretty "straight," as we called our relatives, neighbours and old friends who did not embrace the hippie lifestyle.

It is my own belief that when all those who became his first students seemed to be from the counter-culture, Syd tried to accommodate us by changing his wardrobe a bit, becoming more casual and even growing his hair a bit longer. Barb would occasionally wear long skirts like the rest of us, but basically, they kept their home and family with honest, hard-working middle-class values.

Was there the "sweet smell of marijuana?" Well, if so, it probably emanated from our clothing as we celebrated the coming evening with a visit out back of the Hall. Also, the entire local counter-culture population had probably attended and toked up beforehand, as they did for any concert or gathering.

What did this mean? I think Syd came to believe in that moment that the view by the general public of the hippies surrounding him had gotten in the way of his message, and getting the message heard was what he cared about most. So Syd made it known to us in no uncertain terms. His message, essentially, was "Go and get a life!"

It was all over! With the appearance of that letter in the *Driftwood*, our little Woodstock nation would finally collapse for good.

So, hippiedom was *out*, and middle class values were *in*! This was not difficult for Bill and me; truth be told, we actually felt like fake hippies anyway. Although we lived in the little cottage in the woods, eschewed television, sold my furniture when we left the city and lounged around our living-room on the shag carpet in front of our funky stone fireplace built by a red-haired, guitar-playing draft dodger, we still kept some of our former straight ways. We had a washer and dryer, a shower and a bathtub, never went on social assistance, and sent our son to regular school each day, rather than home-schooling him. These were all considered a bit crass and a sign of weakness by the real back-to-the-landers. We truly admired Jim and Judy, who actually delivered their first child in the tepee!

When the edict came down from above, Bill and I re-invented ourselves as quickly as we had become hippies when we moved to the Island. One of my favourite stories was the time we had gone to visit Syd and Barb for tea. It was late fall by now, so I wore a new knitted hat I had found at the local thrift shop. It was lovely, with green and white stripes. Also, it had an opening on each side for my ears or hair to poke through. Had never had a hat like that before! For some reason, our appearance at the front door and into the kitchen drew gales of hearty laughter from Syd and Barb, but mostly from old Mary. She broke up in peals of laughter, which was so at odds with her dignified British background.

"What are you doing with that tea-cozy on your head?!"

More insane laughter by them all. Okay, I had purchased a tea-cozy, but hey, my family were German; no pots of tea, no tea-cozies. We drank strong coffee in big mugs. Actually, it turned out it was *their* tea-cozy that Mary had only just recently donated along with a few other unused household items to the shop who supported our local small hospital. I later discovered a wonderful Indian cotton skirt which I had purchased with red and yellow embroidery in long diagonals was actually someone's duvet. No wonder it had all those buttons along one side.

I actually believe Syd was relieved for a reason to "encourage" us all to go back to living with middle class values, and with the publicity that came with articles in the *Driftwood* about his event, it was a relief to abandon our more outrageous hippie ways and just dress in jeans and tees like other islanders our age.

So, it was back to normal. The following week, in the September 3, 1975 issue of the *Gulf Islands Driftwood*, eight Letters to the Editor appeared concerning the Beaver Point talk. Six were by students of Syd, with captions such as "That Hate Filled Editor" and "Peace and Wisdom," with one written by Mary Simpson. One, written by a Roy Hamilton of Washington, D.C. who was apparently in the audience, called the previous week's article "hate-filled," and I quote, "I have a very strong feeling like hundreds of others on this island the 'observer' himself was none other than the Editor of the *Driftwood*."

This one was pretty strange, as no one I knew or ever spoke to thought it had been the popular editor of the local paper, and no one I knew had ever met or heard of Roy Hamilton. I always wondered if someone with a grudge against the Editor had sent this under a nom-de-plume.

One of the six letters by students was signed, "Bill Goddu, August 28, 1975." I have always felt a bit strange about this, and Bill still has qualms about it whenever it appears, which it rarely does — thank heavens! A day or so after the blistering piece by "Observer," Syd appeared at our door in a very dour mood. He handed Bill a piece of paper with a Letter to the Editor written on it and asked Bill if he would submit it to the *Driftwood* under Bill's name. Bill hesitated, but not for long. We had all felt angry and betrayed by the article, especially because we knew we were going to have to drop the bongos and willowing. Also, this was a special request from our beloved teacher and guide. It seemed like the right thing to do. The letter, entitled "Love and Hate" by the newspaper, began:

Sir: I hope you realize you condemed (sic) your own report-ers' article when you condemed Syd Banks in last week's edition of the Driftwood.

It was you who sent a reporter to Sydney for a period of three weeks and you who helped write the story. It was an article filled with love. Now you publish a story full of hate and pettiness. It doesn't make sense. Which one are you, hate or love?

Everything your anonymous friend wrote was untrue...

Sydney Banks has changed the lives of many who even psy-chologists and doctors have failed. He is a loving, beautiful person who teaches exactly what Jesus taught, "Truth."

To your anonymous friend who must live in hell, Jesus would say, "Forgive him, Father, he knows not what he says."

Bill Goddu, Box 552, Ganges August 28th, 1975.

137

CHAPTER 21

BACK TO NORMAL?

"Observer" got his wish. We all became "industrious, self-supporting, clean-living citizens" — at least most of us.

Perhaps the news to go straight gave Bill his next great idea. As we walked down the street in downtown Vancouver one day, suddenly out of the blue Bill began to propose! How exciting! As we walked along he began to talk about our relationship. I wasn't sure where this was going, but it sounded like a real commitment.

Just then, we passed a shop with an old wood cook stove in the window, like the one my Granny had on the farm in Saskatchewan. We stopped to have a good look, and Bill, after exclaiming how we should get one of these, forgot he was proposing. I nudged him and he finished, but it was rather lame and there was no big diamond ring. Oh, well, wouldn't have wanted one anyway.

So, early in 1976 we decided to get married. As it was the second time around for us both, we decided to go to the local Courthouse, with two witnesses and $10 to get married. However, it was not to be; countless friends were appalled we weren't going to share this happy day, and told us it was not for us but for our friends and family that we needed to have a nice, big ceremony.

We went to the Catholic Church, of course, but were scared off when the priest learned we had both been married before. It seemed we would have to get special permission from the Bishop in Vancouver, as I had been excommunicated. Then someone told us, "Go to the United Church. They'll marry anyone." So, we met with the minister there, Reverend Vern and when we told him we had both been married before, he hesitated as he took down our names, but only for a second. Then he smiled and said brightly, "Oh well, we all make mistakes. And would you like my wife to play the organ as you come down the aisle?"

What a wedding! It was the first big Sydney Banks-related wedding. Probably once a month for the next year or so another couple would follow our lead and we began to call him "marryin' Vern." We married in April of 1976 and I, with hair done up and in a long off-white gown, came down the aisle on the arm of Sydney Banks, all dressed up in suit and tie. Bill had on a very expensive custom suit from the most high-end shop in downtown Vancouver, and even little Gary had a nice little brown pant suit with brown oxfords. He never again would wear this outfit, but I guess he knew not to raise a fuss on the big day.

Kim Carragher, another student and dear friend, played the guitar and sang, "Our House," one of our favourite tunes. Other friends picked hundreds, maybe thousands of golden daffodils, which grew in every meadow and old homestead on the Island. Wonderful photos from that day show all of us, no longer hippies but with warm, wonderful smiles helping us to celebrate. They all chipped in to buy us a television. Now, we were really straight! And off to Southern California we went for a Honeymoon. We even did Disneyland!

Sheri:

The early '70s were sort of "anti-establishment" and a

lot of us demonstrated this with long hair, beards, giving our children "far-out" names like Rainbow and Tree. Syd gave a talk one day on how cruel it was to use names that made children get teased and not fit in. That we didn't have to try to be different: "Just be ordinary people. Be a family. Love and enjoy each other and your children."

Suddenly, hair was getting shorter, beards were shaved and many of us that had been living common-law got married. Don and I were married in 1977 and Syd gave the toast at our wedding. I remember many things about that day, but Syd saying, "I know Don and Sheri will be happy because they have heard the truth," is ingrained in my memory. However, many friends and family not from the group looked quite puzzled.

Besides getting married and putting all the kids in school, we all went into business. One of the most exciting ventures was that Jim Wallace opened the first full-time law practice on Saltspring. Previously, we only had a visiting lawyer once a week. Jim's partner was another young lawyer, Brian Lercher, who had heard Syd speak in Vancouver and moved to the Island. And their legal secretary was *me*! Now I donned a nice dress each day, along with high heels, and went to the office.

"Observer" was probably stunned. The fellows rented the largest, most expensive office in a new building project just completed on the edge of town. And, they let *me* decorate it! Lovely gold carpet, wallpaper was the rage back then and I chose a lovely gold striped very expensive pattern. When someone entered, there I sat, all dressed up, with my desk in the large reception area. Jim and Brian both had separate offices, and mostly did wills and real estate conveyancing. I don't think we had any crime back then.

Jim and Judy left the tepee and moved into the most incredible home anyone had ever seen, designed by another Syd student and built by Seagull Construction, which Jim Beck, Bill Carragher and several other students formed to build houses.

Bill formalized his carpentry jobs into an entity we called Heritage Construction, our motto being "Homes of Distinction." He hired a crew and ultimately built around fifteen large custom waterfront homes, including one for us. I had seen a gorgeous picture of a Tudor cottage in a magazine. "Can you build this?" I asked. "Sure," Bill replied, cocky as hell. He had never built a house before! It turned out to have the most complicated beam structure anyone had ever seen, including a venerable old British trained carpenter who actually instructed Bill on how to build it.

Edith Sacker, an older lady who also had heard Syd in Vancouver and moved to Saltspring, opened up the first full-time accounting office. Harry Derbitsky, who'd also moved over with wife Cindy, ran the insurance office. Michelle Grant, who took most of the pictures in *Island of Knowledge*, opened up a photography studio and shop. Sandra Clapham purchased and ran the local flower shop. I can't remember them all, but soon there were more businesses and shops run by us "industrious, self-supporting, clean-living citizens" than you could count. Syd was immeasurably pleased with us all.

With *Island of Knowledge* gaining a lot of publicity a local lady who had come to a few meetings and owned the book and stationery shop asked me if I could do a reading and book-signing downtown. Of course I said yes. More high profile Sydney Banks news. Word of anything any of us did seemed to fly around the Island in hours or days.

Were the locals happy that we were now upstanding citizens? Not at all! Anything anyone did in business or in their private lives was now scrutinized, criticized or commented on. Looking back, I can see how when we became more high-profile we might have scared people even more than when we were stoned hippies lying around the nude beach.

Besides getting married and building the lovely Tudor home on the water, more exciting things were happening in my life than I could keep track of. Bill and I were travelling around Vancouver Island to Victoria, Courtenay, Nanaimo, and other spots to deliver books to any and every book shop on Vancouver Island. Locally, Sydney Banks had become a household word, and the books were flying off the shelves. Atman Books in downtown Victoria was the spiritual bookshop of note, and they sold hundreds of copies for us.

Even more exciting was the day Banyen Books took *Island of Knowledge*. They were and still are, I believe, the foremost spiritual book shop and center for all things spiritual and Buddhist in British Columbia and were involved in organizing Gathering of the Ways. They sold more books than I could ever have imagined, and soon, almost all of our printing of two thousand was gone.

Even more exciting, Syd and I began our next book. Now we had more confidence this was really going to happen. Syd was becoming a household word in B.C. with visitors appearing and requesting interviews constantly. As his fame spread and he became much busier, now with hundreds of students instead of just one — or eight, or even twenty — our time together became greatly curtailed.

No more long afternoons at the kitchen table. Syd

would drop by or call me over and hand me his latest writings, and I sensed things were shifting and changing. Work on the second book proceeded much more slowly, even as Syd felt an even greater need for his work to now be available to all. Rather than the slow lovely days in the meadow, with my working full-time and more and more demands on Syd, it was truly a different experience.

The teachings were less personal. To this day, I can't decide which book I like better. They seem to me both so different, for *Beyond Beliefs* was written in such a different spiritual, social and intellectual climate than *Island of Knowledge*. I love them both, I suppose, in very different ways. As we began work on it, *Beyond Beliefs* seemed to me to be a lot more universal in nature—less personal, and most of it was beyond my comprehension.

Linda, Bill and Gary at wedding

CHAPTER 22

THE THREE PRINCIPLES

Almost two years had now passed since my first meeting with Syd, and just as Syd had predicted, I was only the first of many. He assured me from the beginning that someday his name and teachings would be renowned; that I, too, would be world famous as I presented his teachings with my books and writing. It was my destiny, he said, and I believed him.

By 1976 both our lives had changed dramatically. Syd now spoke regularly in Vancouver, Victoria, Mayne Island, Courtenay and other locations. He travelled constantly. At each of his talks, which we all attended to support Syd, several or perhaps a dozen or so people who had been searching for something and were spellbound by Syd's talks would move to the Island.

Another development that began around this time was the taping of Syd's talks. I can't believe to this day how many truly mystical and life-changing words had been spoken by this quiet man with his soft Scottish brogue that have been lost forever. With Bill's experience as roadie with the rock n' roll band, he became Syd's first tape man. From now on, each talk was captured on tape, and now after four decades students are once again hearing some of these incredible talks which represented a breakthrough in human consciousness.

Early in the year a small group had formed in Victoria, B.C. and, as I recall, they met regularly at the home of

Larry and Chris Colero. Many of these students would later move to the Island. Victoria was special in that it had been one of few Canadian cities that had the privilege of having world-renowned spiritual teacher, Joel Goldsmith of *The Infinite Way* visit and speak there often. Goldsmith spent decades travelling the globe and lecturing, has several hundred tapes available and around thirty-five books published of his teachings. Joel had chosen two or three teachers to carry on his teachings, and one lived in Victoria: Eileen Bowden.

As Joel visited Victoria in the '50s and '60s until his passing in 1964, a very large group of his students had formed there. Many came to Syd's talks when they learned that an enlightened man was speaking at various venues. Almost since the beginning, when Syd spoke anywhere besides his living room, the rest of us would mingle with the crowd, asking them how they had heard about Syd, if they had any questions, and just generally sharing. This is how I learned that dozens of people came from The Infinite Way group.

The Infinite Way people had no problem with their students studying other teachings, reading other philosophies, as this freedom had been granted by Joel to his students. Syd knew of Joel's teachings, as I recall both of us reading one day the quotation on illumination in the front of each of Joel's books.

At one point, some of these students asked if Syd could speak at one of their weekly meetings, which took place each Sunday in a downtown hotel, the old Sussex, where they had been meeting since the 1950s. Syd agreed and was in process of arranging a date when a message came from Eileen Bowden, who still led the Victoria group, that this would not be possible.

Perhaps because I had met so many Infinite Way students and also had met Eileen I became the go-between between Eileen and Syd. Knowing forty or fifty of their students were coming to his talks, Syd was furious that his talk with their group should be cancelled. He said to me, incredulously, "I can't believe they would prefer listening to a tape of a long-dead enlightened man, when they could have a real live enlightened man speak to them!"

Eileen explained to me that although perhaps forty or fifty of the group wished Syd to come to their meeting and speak, another forty or fifty did not want him to speak and, after all, as she pointed out, it *was* an Infinite Way meeting. After a lot of discussion Syd invited Eileen to come to visit on Saltspring and they would discuss things. She agreed and I was to meet her at the ferry and bring her over to Syd and Barb's.

I remember it was a lovely spring day, and we three sat in the meadow on the lawn chairs while Barb served tea and cookies. After explaining things to Syd, Eileen added that so many of the students who had heard Syd did not want him to speak at their meetings because they just couldn't relate to his style of teaching.

The talk went back and forth, and eventually Syd asked why they couldn't relate when they were all staunch followers of Joel who basically taught the same thing. Eileen explained that feedback from these people, who had perhaps been at one or two talks, was that Syd's style of teaching was that one would just listen and they would get it.

"There is no structure!" said Eileen.

I don't remember all the conversation word-for-word, of course, but I do remember that statement perfectly. Isn't that what we *loved* about Syd's teaching? Perhaps it was that most of the Infinite Way students were a couple of decades older than most of us in the group.

"Structure?" Syd sounded puzzled and quite dubious.

"Yes," Eileen went on to explain. "In the Infinite Way, Joel has three principles, which one can read, study and ponder, thus leading to a deeper understanding."

She didn't go into detail, but Joel's three principles are:

1) The Nature of God -   Our innermost being.

2) The Nature of Prayer -   Inner contemplation, not
                            asking God for something.

3) The Nature of Error -   Sin is error, or wrong thinking,
                            or something of the sort.

I didn't really understand those principles, but I know that every one of Joel's books talks about those three principles over and over, explaining them in great detail. I think entire books were written by Joel explicating these principles he had discovered during his experiences.

We all had a pleasant chat, and I drove Eileen back to the ferry. How surprised I was, a couple of weeks later, when next I heard Syd speak, that he had discovered Three Principles that explained everything: Mind, Consciousness and Thought.

It is often believed that Syd discovered these principles with his initial experience. But in the beginning he didn't really use those terms at all. He spoke mostly about energy. His definition of God, when asked, was always "the energy of all things." He didn't speak about consciousness in the beginning, so much as "levels of consciousness." He spoke endlessly about these levels. Your level was the most important thing. Often, as I recall, he would share with us what he thought about *our* level, whether we liked it or not, but we learned *so* much!

He did speak about thought, but mostly about our thoughts, such as our thoughts about the past, the future; our negative thoughts.

Did Syd co-opt someone else's concepts and ideas? I once read a book that Joel Goldsmith recommended to his students, written in the late 1800s and discovered many of the words and terms Joel used. I never had the idea that Syd leaned on someone else's material. Most of what Syd shared with us in the beginning was so fresh, new and different that it was incomprehensible to most people.

But I could see, as Syd spoke more and more publicly and as the crowds really began to come in earnest, that Syd knew he had to move away from the personal and teach in a way more people could relate to. I think our next book would reflect this, as he moved into a beautiful, mystical and more universal teaching.

CHAPTER 23

THINGS FALL APART

Perhaps the pinnacle of the Sydney Banks movement on Saltspring Island occurred in May 1978, when the following article appeared in the *Gulf Islands Driftwood*, written by none other than Frank Richards, the *Driftwood* editor whom Syd believed had written the devastating "observer" article. If so, he had doubtlessly been impressed when we indeed turned into "industrious, self-supporting, clean-living citizens."

I present here most, but not all, of the two articles. The complete versions can be read on the *Gulf Islands Driftwood* archives on that date.[8]

MAN WITH MANY FOLLOWERS
SYDNEY BANKS IS PART OF THE ISLANDS NOW

Sydney Banks is part of the fabric of Salt Spring Island.

Bearded like the Messiah, he has piercing brown eyes and the quiet voice of a dreamer. Yet, he is not dreamer, he avers. Rather, God is the dreamer and we are His reality, suggests the Prophet of St. Mary Lake.

The message of brotherly love which Sydney Banks has carried for better than three years is the message of God, he is convinced.

Quietly, almost too quietly at times, he explains himself. He delivers the words, but the message comes from a conviction

---

deep within him. Once he had no conviction.

Life was tedious, although at the time he believed himself to be happy. In those days he was employed as a welder, a task he loathed. He suffered from a complete and utter lack of confidence. He could not get up and speak three consecutive words for nervousness. And his marriage was teetering and both he and his wife, Barbara knew it.

A Scot who crossed the Atlantic to live and work in Canada, he still wears his brogue like a Scots shipbuilder. Everything else has changed.

HAPPY AND OUTGOING

His marriage is happy and firm; he has abandoned his work in the steel business and he scarcely remembers what it is to be self-conscious. None of these changes came without effort.

Some years ago Sydney and Barbara Banks were aware of the lack of harmony between them. They both knew he was dissatisfied and uncertain. And they also knew that his health was beginning to fail.

So they took an awareness group. The man against whom he was paired asked what his problems were. Banks explained that he was nervous and uncertain of himself, among other things. Later, walking on the beach, his new-found friend commented, "You say you are insecure! I never heard of so much rubbish in all my life!

"There is no insecurity," Sydney Banks assured me last week. "It's all in your mind."

That was his first spiritual encounter. For three days and nights he was awake, he recalls. His mind was undergoing a transformation. Life, the world was filled with beauty that was his awareness and his only concern. The third night...he found himself completely shrouded in 'living energy.'

"I had found the secret of life!" He would be writing books, speaking to thousands, he assured her. Time was to prove him right. He had lost his insecurity. His sense of being always lost. He had learned peace of mind and he had gained the urge to pass it on to others. He was no longer ailing and quarrelling with his wife.

He doesn't boast. He is utterly and completely convinced of an empathy with his Maker. Call him teacher: call him preacher. It matters little. Sydney Banks is a mild-mannered man who found himself and who is satisfied he found the answer to the ills of mankind at the same time.

* * *

STORY OF AN ISLAND MOVEMENT[9]

Neither preacher nor teacher, Sydney Banks is the leader of a new brotherhood of living in harmony. He talks and others listen. And those who listen remain to apply to their own lives the principles outlined by the former welder.

His followers identify Sydney Banks with the change in their lives that made them into sound, happy citizens after a period of uncertainty and strife and fear. Only by virtue of his help are they able to take their place in their various communities as good living, good citizens.

In this, or any other community: for the Sydney Banks Foundation has extended far beyond the boundaries of Saltspring Island.

There are followers of the 'enlightened man' in other parts of Canada, in California and elsewhere in the United States

---

[9] *Gulf Islands Driftwood,* May 24, 1978.

and in Australia. There are many followers of the modern-day prophet in business on Saltspring Island. Having come here, some find work. Others find small businesses.

But, don't get fooled! There's no money in the business of leading people into the light! The Island is full of rumours of big donations by wealthy American doctors. It's rubbish! The Sydney Banks Foundation has some money. It is given by supporters of the movement who feel they owe more than they can repay.

In March some 50 members of the psychology and associated professions in the Pacific Northwest attended a seminar at Cedar Beach Resort. In June, there will be a further seminar on Saltspring Island of those engaged in the helping professions. But there is no big money changing hands.

The Sydney Banks Foundation on Saltspring Island lists some 120 adult members. That brings it into the strength of most island churches in terms of numbers. It brings it into a greater strength, perhaps, in terms of fervour, conviction and acceptance.

The Sydney Banks Foundation is a power in the community. It has brought many unhappy, confused, uncertain people to Saltspring Island and turned them into good-living, warmly accepted members of the community.

So you don't really understand their philosophy? So what? It doesn't matter. What really matters is that the mild-mannered little Scot has brought something to the life of the Island that has made a very valuable contribution to our society here.

* * *

Recently, a lovely lady from Britain who came to visit

Saltspring and attend the Three Principles School here called and asked if we could go for tea together. We met at our favourite local café on the water, just down from Syd's old place, and chatted for hours. I hope she enjoyed it as much as I.

She told me one thing had been bothering her. She had heard that at one time the Island was full of Syd's followers and that suddenly he had ordered them all to leave. This, she felt, was really arrogant and made her wonder about Syd's control over his students.

I explained to her that, indeed, it was not arrogant at all. The Island had become overrun with people moving here to follow Syd and be part of our group. By this time there well may have been one hundred students here. As hippies, I believe we just kind of blended in with all the other back-to-the-landers like ourselves, but once we went into business and became those industrious, self-supporting, clean-living citizens, I believe we became very, very visible and not always in a positive way.

One day, Syd invited us for tea and said he had something he wished to speak with us about. This usually meant, "Uh, oh!" But he let us know it was nothing serious and we'd just have a nice visit. The local hardware store in town was for sale, and Syd thought it would be a good idea if Bill and I bought and ran it. We kind of looked at each other in disbelief.

"Well, no!" we said. Bill was really happy in the building trades, and Heritage Construction was now considered one of the top three companies on the Island and he had a permanent crew of three carpenters to help. Heritage was always asked to bid on the best custom homes. I was totally happy working with the boys at the law office.

It was one of the most prestigious jobs on the Island at that time, and I was told I was the third highest paid lady on Saltspring, after the school secretary and the head lady in the local government office. Pretty glamourous working with these two handsome dudes, and I couldn't see myself selling rat traps or hammers.

So, we politely declined Syd's suggestion and told him we were making more money than we had ever dreamed of and were both really happy in our work. He looked a little disappointed, but didn't say much.

So many people got married and went into business that perhaps at one time fully one half of the businesses on Saltspring and especially the highly-visible downtown area were being run by "Sydney Bankers."

All that notwithstanding, as I said, Syd was incredibly generous. I recall a hippie friend in the group who had been invited to a wedding, but didn't have anything appropriate to wear. He ran into Syd in town one day, with Syd sporting a nice brown suede jacket. When our friend admired it, Syd promptly took it off and handed it to Brian. "Here," he said, "it's yours!" "I couldn't possibly keep it," said Brian. "Don't be silly," said Syd, or something to that effect. "Take it!" That was Syd.

To obtain a mortgage to build our lovely new homes or to start a business it was often necessary to go to the local Credit Union to obtain a loan. However, bedraggled hippies were not likely to obtain enough for a used car. Syd, by now, had purchased a nice, white suit—not the hippie guru type, but an actual business suit for his more formal talks. One of the fellows heading to the interview for his loan hit upon the bright idea of asking Syd to lend him the nice white suit. I'm sure he looked impressive. It worked so well, someone else did the same. Bill had his nice outfit with navy blue sports coat from our wedding, so he wore that for our interview. We laughed when the manager in the loans department said, "The white suit has been here in my office four times this week!"

Would "observer" have liked this? Not sure. Remember that small Oregon town where the New Age guru had seventeen Rolls Royces? His students took over the schools and businesses just by sheer numbers. Just as this caused pandemonium, law suits and court cases in Oregon, the locals on Saltspring began to freak out at our sheer numbers.

Adding to the problem was the fact that many of us did not have a clue what we were doing. I had about twelve years experience as an executive assistant, but Bill had never built houses and there were times when we made huge mistakes. We lost so much on one job we had to put a small mortgage on our new home, but with lots of hard work we managed to pay it off.

Others were not so lucky, and so businesses began to falter and many of them then failed. Lots of businesses fail, but we had been so high-profile that it was more and more obvious that we "Sydney Bankers" were around in huge numbers and still causing trouble.

There were a couple of lawsuits—I'm not sure if Syd ever knew about them—but several of these businesses went out with a big bang. Also, as Syd's travels increased and more visitors came to the Island to meet with and hear him, he became probably the most well-known citizen here.

During these years, the growing movement also attracted many, many visitors to hear Syd speak. Now we were renting a local resort on the lake which had a huge meeting room and guests could stay at the resort and others spread around the lakeshore.

Sheri:

I remember Cedar Beach. Syd gave a talk one night when we were having our meetings there. It was dark and rainy out and everybody in the audience was kind of relaxed and mesmerized — that meditative state one got into when Syd was speaking.

The door rattled and burst open. The rain came in, and this soaking wet fellow came in. We didn't know his name. He started asking in quite a loud voice who we were, what was happening and what we were meeting about? It felt quite disruptive, brought you out of that reverie and it was upsetting. People started to shush him and get him to leave.

And Syd said, "NO! Wait! He's here for a reason!"

Then Syd asked him what was happening. And the guy, who was very upset, said, "My mother just died tonight!" He was crying, and Syd started to speak just to him. I remember some of the things he said.

"There is no such thing as death," was one thing he said.

"The energy of all things will always exist," was another.

Syd talked to him for quite a while and some of the things I just didn't understand but it was quite soothing to me, and very soothing to the guy. The man stayed for the rest of the meeting, and he calmed down and told us how much Syd's talk had helped him and that he was going to miss his mom, but he understood something now and he didn't understand what it was. He had coffee and snacks

with us at the end of the night and we all gave him hugs.
We never saw him again.

* * *

These were the years when the "psychologists"
arrived, so this growing phenomena of more people visiting received vastly more publicity. In his book, *Paradigm
Shift*[10], Jack Pransky details most of these events, and on
page 88 describes the arrival of Val, who as I recall was the
first of many people from afar who were destined to
change the entire direction of Syd's teachings and events
on Saltspring.

Syd was now so busy that even though we had begun
the new book I was lucky to see him once a week or so
and spend a couple of hours with him, and this was probably more time than he spent with other students. With
Val's arrival, something shifted. Syd spent hours a day
with him, and we were all puzzled and a little jealous, I
think. We weren't quite sure what was happening, but it
looked like all of us loyal students from the early days
were being edged out by more important people.

But as more and more therapists, psychologists, psychiatrists and those in the helping professions appeared —
Roger Mills, George Pransky and others — we realized this
was a natural progression of the growth of Syd's teaching.
This is what Syd had predicted all along, that his teachings
would one day be taught in universities and colleges, used
in business, in medicine, in prisons and other institutions,
where not dozens but tens of thousands of people would
share in the benefits of meeting and hearing a "man of

---

[10] *Paradigm Shift* (2015). Jack Pransky. British Columbia: CCB Publishing

knowledge."

The arrival of Dr. Roger C. Mills would prove to be a seminal event on the Island. Roger may have been a practicing psychologist and a professional, but he also had long hair and a beard. Hurray, he was one of us!

Roger instantly became friends with us all, and there was no separation between him and the rest of us. Roger came over to watch movies, sat on the beach with us, and always in my memory I will remember the evening he invited Bill and I over for dinner. With dessert he brought out a glass pot with a strange looking plastic filter with a paper liner, ground up some coffee beans in an actual coffee grinder and made us our first cup of dark roast coffee. It was an epiphany and we were very impressed with his sophisticated ways.

Roger, I believe, along with George Pransky, was the catalyst for the new paradigm where mental health professionals would come, listen to Syd, and accept and adopt his teachings. Roger helped to bridge the gap between these two vastly different groups of people, and soon, as more therapists and those in the helping professions arrived and as our original group became more straight and went back to work, we all melded seamlessly into one larger body of students.

Jim Wallace:

> *From almost our first meeting with Syd, he had predicted repeatedly that eventually word of what was happening to us would reach the upper levels of the helping professions, particularly in the mental health field, and that sooner or later one of them would "see." He always gave "seeing" a special meaning in this context, and I took it to mean understanding what he was talking about.*

When the first psychologists arrived from the United States, few of us realized the significance of the event. We all took an immediate liking to them and their many associates that followed, but at the time they were to me only the latest of countless others who had arrived for the same purpose. Their presence, however, was to mark another great change in our lives. Almost immediately, Syd was called to shift his attention to the United States, but that is another story.

Sheri:

In 1979, through a connection with psychiatrists and psychologists in the USA, Syd was able to focus his teachings in that direction. The group had been growing too large and people were actually moving to Saltspring Island to be near Syd. He kept telling us, "The answers lie within you." He didn't want us to start to worship and idolize him. Syd said that was a problem with many religions that have started with the words of enlightened people but have gotten lost in the beliefs, ceremonies and worship outside of self. I think he saw that beginning to happen and he needed to take his work in a different direction. I felt he was telling me to stop looking to him for the answers and live an ordinary life, doing good and sharing knowledge in my own way.

The arrival of these professionals occurred about the same time as businesses began to implode on Saltspring. What a time! It was exciting, no doubt about that. But after one large gathering at Cedar Beach Resort, which the Foundation almost purchased as a meeting center, Syd went to town and had a very unfortunate encounter.

Walking down the street with Barb, a lady obviously not friendly came roaring up and began shouting at him. I recall Syd's recollection of the event.

"Your People! Your People!" she shouted over and over. It appeared she was the owner of a local resort where dozens of people had stayed for Syd's last talk. Apparently, they had walked off with towels, toilet paper rolls, ashtrays, and anything else they could remove.

"My People?" inquired Syd in a huff! "My People? I give a talk and I am responsible for anyone from anywhere who comes to hear me?"

I think this conversation went on for a few minutes, with each of them telling each other off, but again this event led to big changes. Syd at the time was running into this kind of negativity almost anywhere he appeared on Saltspring.

Jim Beck recalled a similar incident when I spoke to him for this book. "Jim," I had queried, going into a kind of touchy subject, "Sydney Banks became a very controversial figure on Saltspring Island, and for some of us, being his student brought with it problems at work and other issues. How did you experience this?"

Jim Beck:

> *Lots of people did not accept Syd. My mom said — based on your book* Island of Knowledge, *which had a chapter entitled, "I Meet a Prophet" — "He's not a prophet!" She came to visit and we were walking down the street and I introduced her to Syd. She said, "I'll not shake your hand," and walked across the street and left us both hanging. When this happened, as it often did, I just accepted that not everyone was ready. As Syd often said, "We react to the truth according to our own level of consciousness. Some are frightened, some are thrilled, some are terrified, and some are elevated!"*

But, Syd had had enough!

Okay. It was all over, like the Willowing. Did he kick everyone off Saltspring? Well, not exactly, because Bill and I didn't go, and neither did a few others, but Syd made it very clear that people needed to go and get a life. Basically, Syd's public life on Saltspring was over.

Today, it is only a very, very rare occurrence when someone on the Island remembers Sydney Banks or *Island of Knowledge*.

CHAPTER 24

"YOU'RE FIRED!"

Not only had Sydney Banks become a household word on the Island, but Syd began to travel further afield to spread his message. In mid-to-late 1977 Syd travelled more and more, to Oregon where Dr. Roger Mills lived, and to California where George Pransky lived.

By now *Island of Knowledge* had sold almost its entire run of 2,000 copies. Someone at the time said that 5,000 was a Canadian Best-Seller, so I should be proud. Lately, another friend in publishing said in the late 1970s that 2,000 *was* a Canadian Best-Seller. Obviously, with its success, the demand for another book of Syd's writings became a priority.

But, with Syd constantly either on the road or working with visiting professionals in the helping field, our time together became less and less. Often, he would just hand me his latest writings, without even an hour or two to go over them together with my questions as we had in the past.

Also, we had had an argument or two about the second book; something that had never happened before. Syd began to make suggestions, and even on occasion demanded something be included. Previously he had just handed me his writings and let me work them into form, and he had always been delighted with my work. Now, he insisted I include a story about one young woman who'd had a wonderful experience; however, something felt suspect to me about her exciting narrative, so I declined to include it.

Another time, Syd wished me to write a chapter devoted to one family who'd had major problems prior to meeting him. Joe (not his real name) had not been work-ing, and his wife was depressed with two little kids and the other usual problems. Now Joe seemed highly success-ful. But I didn't want to tell Syd the local gossip that they were deeply in debt, that one prominent couple with whom Joe had been working were taking him to court over something that had gone horribly wrong in their business relationship. Syd would not have liked this. So, I refused to do that chapter also, without going into detail.

Things had changed so much. Jim Wallace and Brian Lercher decided to close the Law Office. It appeared there was indeed only enough work for one part-time lawyer on the Island, and after they had done wills for everyone, they just didn't have enough business. So, I was also out of a job.

Edith Sacker, who had moved from Vancouver after hearing Syd speak at the Planetarium there, opened up an accounting office directly across the street from Wallace & Lercher. She offered me a job, and I worked there for three or four years part-time until I quit working permanently to run my own business.

One evening in January 1978 Syd called to say he was having a get-together at the Banks' home. As I recall, this was one of the coldest winters in history on Saltspring. Even the lake froze over, which has never occurred since. Strangely, I recently found an old diary from those days, which I apparently only kept for about three months. But, it detailed a fateful day in January. My entry for January 15th is as follows:

"This week, Seven Swans A-Swimming passed by the house. They were such an incredible sight! Three white and four grey. The cold has created a totally different landscape, frosted and icy!

"Well, this last week has surely been eventful, if not enjoyable. We arrived at Syd's to find about sixteen people sitting around the living room, but Syd seemed angry at me. Bill and I were stunned; we didn't know what was going on. Syd said I was not into the book and it is off! I have been so afraid to write something wrong; I tried to write exactly what he told me, and ended up writing almost nothing. But, I am also a bit relieved!"

We arrived at Syd's that Friday evening a bit late. I had rushed home from work, made dinner—I always cooked a full meal for Bill and Gary, who was about twelve at the time. Then rushed off to Syd's to find a dozen cars in the drive and we were about the last to arrive. Syd came to the door, greeted us, and I took off my nice new suede coat and tossed it on the pile by the door.

"Where's the book?" asked Syd.

I hesitated. The book? Syd had not told me, as he always did, that it was a "book night" and I should bring the manuscript. The process with the second book was so different than the way in which *Island of Knowledge* had developed. Now, with the success of the first book, and the growing movement around Sydney Banks, a new routine followed whenever I had finished a chapter.

The pattern now was for me to bring over a finished chapter, and the tape machine would be set up. Barb Banks would sit in front next to the tape machine, and in her soft but strong voice, read the chapter to a hushed room. There might only be a dozen or so people, and I believe we all knew that it was now an honour and a privilege to be invited to these infrequent evenings.

"The book?" I asked. "I didn't bring it. It's not quite finished and I didn't have time to type it out. It's just written by hand."

Syd became quite angry and raised his voice. "You should have brought it regardless!"

I was stunned, but there was more. Boy, he was angry! Bill stood beside me, also stunned, with Barb behind Syd looking a bit alarmed herself. Well, after a couple of minutes of this I turned, picked up my coat, and prepared to exit stage left. Suddenly, Syd changed completely, came over and took my coat.

"That's okay," he said in his usual calm voice, "Come on in. We'll do it next time."

We walked into the living room where everyone sat as usual on cushions on the floor, and they all looked as scared as I probably did. My dear friend Sandy spoke up in my defense, bless her.

"Syd, we almost never see Bill and Linda anymore. She's just so busy working on that book, even on the weekends. I know she's putting her heart and soul into it!"

"Who asked you?" demanded Syd. Sandy looked taken aback. She and Larry were two old friends from Syd's and Barb's days in Nanaimo and Larry also had worked at the pulp mill with Syd.

The room was deadly quiet. No one dared speak. Barb moved and Syd took his place at the front, began to speak, and soon things were back to normal. We had coffee at the break, and Syd came up and asked me to stay after the meeting was over. Uh oh.

"I know it's a lot for you to do," said Syd, a lot more reasonably when we gathered in the kitchen after almost everyone had left. He thought perhaps I needed help, and Barb and perhaps a couple of others could help get the manuscript ready for publication. He talked softly but firmly, and reminded me that people all over the globe were now awaiting these words of wisdom, and it was imperative to get the book out.

I thought for a moment about a "committee" writing the book and decided this would lead to chaos. I reassured Syd that I would put 100% of my time and energy into the book; that, in fact, he would have the finished chapter by Monday. In the future, I assured him, each chapter would be finished promptly, and in fact after fifteen years in the corporate world, I actually worked best under pressure.

Syd seemed to agree, and we left it at that. Bill and I returned home in silence. I wasn't sure what was happening, but I did feel a bit resentful that something was happening I wasn't aware of.

The next morning was brilliant. It had been so cold overnight that the local pond froze over. Brian, who lived near the pond, called to say we could go skating. Brian had skates, Gary had a little pair for school outings to the rink on Vancouver Island, and Bill had been offered skates by the next door neighbour.

The sky was incredibly blue, snow lay piled up around the house and frost glistened from every blade of grass, twig and branch. I had never seen such a sight on the West Coast, more like the cold but brilliant winter days I grew up with on the prairies in Northern Alberta. I was in my element.

Bill, Gary and I stood near the front door, ready to trudge up the hill to the pond, skates in hand, wooly mittens on and laughing at this unusual escapade. We had never skated on the Island before or since. Suddenly, there came a loud knock at the door.

It was Sydney Banks and, as they say, he was not a happy camper. He looked furious, and began to yell at me. Basically, he said I was into my big, fat ego; that with a book published I now thought I was really somebody. How dare I reject help to bring the book to completion? Syd continued that people were waiting in line for an opportunity to work with him the way I had, and I was really ungrateful and taking it all for granted. I had blown it *big time*, and others were now going to work with him, and our book was off!

There was more, but I stood there, transfixed. Frozen with terror! Syd, over the last couple of years, had moved away from the way he had been in the beginning, and those of us close to him realized there was a lot of stress and pressure on him. More and more, he might become angry over small things, and slowly we became afraid to be honest with Syd and tell him certain things that were happening that might make him angry.

I stood there, frozen, conscious of Bill and Gary on each side, all of us silent. I had never been so afraid in my whole life. My worst fears had come to pass. Syd was livid! He spoke more about my ego, and it went on and on.

Suddenly, out of the fear and terror came a different feeling. Subtle at first, then more and more powerful. Syd continued his tirade in a very loud voice, but slowly, he seemed to be growing smaller and smaller, although only two or three feet away. His voice seemed to become very, very quiet, although I could still hear every word.

A strange calm overtook me. I was no longer afraid. In fact, I had never felt so calm or present in my entire life. Finally I found what I had been searching for all my life, since that day in the meadow. I had gone *inside*!

At some point, it may have been five or ten minutes, Syd turned, slammed the door and left. We all stood in stunned silence. But my strange and wonderful feeling continued. And, slowly, the love and admiration I'd always felt for Syd returned. This wonderful man, who had so kindly and graciously given me new life—he was human too! And in that moment I became free! I felt only overwhelming gratitude, and thought, "Syd, I am forever grateful to you!" I had now found happiness from within—exactly what Syd had been talking about for all those years.

"Okay," I said cheerily! "Let's go!"

I picked up my skates where I had dropped them at my feet in panic, and headed out the door and up the hill to Brian's pond. That day it seemed I never skated so well in all my life, and unlike the West Coasters who had not grown up on skates I was a Star on the ice. I twirled and whirled in the sparking sunshine. I did flat-irons, pirouettes and all the fancy tricks that even Bill had never seen me perform. Everyone there was astonished at my skill on ice, and in fact, at one time I had wished to become a professional figure skater. Such a day! Rather than the gloomy clouds of January, the mist and fog; on this special day the universe sparkled and shone. I had never been so happy!

The next week or so proved to be a very interesting time. I learned a lot, like who my friends were. At work on Monday, Edith sympathized with me, told me to just ignore it all, and that I would be fine. Walking uptown one day I saw two of our close friends from the group approaching me on the sidewalk.

I waved and prepared to go up for a chat when they glanced at me, turned, and crossed to the other side of the street. It was my first experience at "shunning" by the group, which I hadn't known about.

I would soon find out. No one called.

Only Sandy and Larry and another couple or two kept in touch. It was one of the most hurtful experiences of my life. I hadn't really thought that not writing the book would mean I was *out*!

On the other hand, no one called.

I felt free. *Free!* I had not realized what a huge responsibility working with Syd on the book had become. That the whole world was waiting for *me*? Waiting on me to deliver Syd's words of wisdom to the hovering masses? Wisdom I knew could change a life, a family, an island? What a burden! I was so glad to be free of it!

Two weeks later at work on Monday morning Edith got a phone call and said she had to go out immediately. No problem, I often took care of the office. Minutes after she left, the door opened and in came Sydney Banks. Uh, oh! I thought. But, it was the old Syd, friendly and smiling.

"I'd like to talk to you," he said.

"I'm really sorry for what happened. I was really out

of line. I want you to come back and finish writing the book."

"It will all be different," he said, "just like in the old days. No more taping the book until it's all finished. Just you and I working on it in private, and keeping it all confidential until it's finished."

I didn't answer. Speechless.

"Well, okay," he said. "Just think it over." He apologized some more, then left.

I didn't need to think it over. The answer was "*No!* Thanks!"

The next Sunday, Bill and I were outside working on the front yard where we planned to put in a lawn come spring. Suddenly Carol appeared and told us cheerily that Syd was having a "work bee" that day and wanted us to come over.

Wow! A personal invitation! That was different. But no, we told her. We were too busy working on the lawn, and with full time jobs it was the only day we got to work on the house and yard, but thanks anyway. I guess we had made a statement, because we never got another invitation to Syd's house.

That was it. No more Sydney Banks. No more book[11]. Best of all, no more group!

---

[11] The book *Beyond Beliefs: The Lost Teachings of Sydney Banks* was finally published in 2016 by CCB Publishing, British Columbia.

CHAPTER 25

THE END

Our small family now settled down to a more ordinary life, just like Syd had wished us all to do. From time to time Syd would appear at the front door, invite himself in for a cup of tea and we would have a nice chat. He never called in advance, so it was all casual and friendly. We never talked about the book again, or the past. Usually, the conversation would center on Syd's travels and talks.

I heard that the book he began with the others was soon scrapped, and a couple of years later Syd decided to write a novel, with his teachings and wisdom embedded in that more entertaining form. He had always wanted to write books. In the coming years he would write several novels, and whenever Syd visited he would bring a signed, autographed copy of his latest book. Soon I might have five or six copies of each and would just pass them along.

The decades passed, three of them, and still we remained friends with Syd until his passing in 2009. Bill and I had finished our lovely Tudor cottage by the sea, and decided to buy a small farm and do more gardening.

We began to keep bees and chickens, then visited the grain farm in Saskatchewan where my father had grown up. It now had heritage status having been farmed by my family since 1907 and my cousin still grew wheat. He gave me a pound, and in the next local Fall Fair we entered a 300-pound pumpkin that Bill grew, and I tied a white satin ribbon around a sheaf of wheat from our small patch. The other guys had just grabbed a sheaf of grain and tied it with a piece of plastic binder twine. We actually won the coveted Farm Trophy-1st Prize-making us the smallest farm ever to win it on Saltspring. Our fate was sealed and we remain farmers to this day.

Years before, as a hippie, I had done what most of us young hippie ladies did; grow herbs and make our own salves, first aid, tinctures and so on. I grew comfrey and made a wonderful healing salve. I gave a jar to my Mom who had arthritis badly in her fingers. She told me it was the first night in years she hadn't awakened with pain. She gave some to her neighbour, who sent me $5.00 for the little brown glass jar of salve. My first sale! Then, her sister sent me $5.00 and out went another jar. Before I knew it, I was sending my salves all across Canada.

How did I get into the handmade soap business? It just happened. One day at the office I found myself looking out the window, just staring into space. I realized I was not doing what I loved. What did I love to do? I loved growing things; herbs and flowers and working in my greenhouse. I had also begun to make bars of handmade soap and my own skin care. Then, a friend asked me to help fill her table at a local Christmas craft fair. The pile of soap I brought as an afterthought went flying out the door. Three decades later, Bill was making soap, Gary was the webmaster while Amber managed our soap shop. We had five shops across B.C., two hundred wholesale accounts and eighteen employees. And I was just doing what I loved!

Syd was so proud of Saltspring Soapworks, and several people later told me that he always admired how practical I was. I think that was a real compliment, even though it sounds pretty boring.

Throughout those decades, a few visits from Syd remain forever etched in my memory. Syd learned Bill and I had joined the local hiking club and with our English Pointer were constantly exploring the forests that surrounded us. Often Syd and his dog, Fergus would come for a walk with us. Mostly, our conversations were about whatever Syd was doing out in the big wide world, and he kept us up to date on what was happening with the teaching he now called The Three Principles.

For those of us who spent time with Sydney Banks in the early years — living, laughing, learning — I believe the transformations we underwent are with us still. Four decades later, as we recall those invigorating days, as memories return, we have all relived some of those amazing times. Not surprisingly, each of us had different insights and experiences in our times with Sydney Banks. His unique, charismatic and ground-breaking teachings left us all with powerful thoughts and feelings. I felt honoured to have my old friends share those memories for this book.

Sheri:

I feel very lucky that Syd came into my life. Hearing him changed my world from a place of fear and anxiety to a place of trust in the flow of life. We've had ups and downs and losses and grief like everyone else, but we know how to tap into the good energy and not stay in those lows.

Jim Beck:

This is about how we all worked and lived together; Syd was an exemplary husband, father and friend. Barb took care of the kids and home and was a role model for us all. They lived what they were teaching, and showed us all the way to have just simple, normal lives – on the outside, while on the inside we were becoming unlike anything else we'd ever experienced!

Jim Wallace:

Nothing could have prepared me for the experience of having a friend like Syd. An aura of peace followed him everywhere he went, and completely enveloped me whenever we met.

Jim Beck:

We felt we were part of the most exciting movement on the planet! We were actually changing and it seemed that many, many others were experiencing the same thing. It was happening! The planet was growing through us! We were on the inside track where an enlightened person discovers his power to share and along with it, he was still half a welder. Syd transitioned from a welder to a world-class teacher of higher-consciousness because he was learning from us how to teach. What worked for people, what they "heard" and how hearing the truth he shared could change the world, just as he had predicted in the moments after his experience.

Sheri:

We know when to "go with the flow" and when to grab the opportunities that come along. I always think about the story of the guy on the roof in the flood. Someone comes along with a raft, another with a boat, and another with a horse.

The guy tells them all, "No, thanks! I have prayed and God will save me."

Of course he drowns and gets to meet God.

He's mad and says, "I have been a good disciple to you, and I prayed and prayed and you didn't save me!"

God says, "Well, I sent you a raft, a boat, a horse..."

Maybe he sent us Syd!

* * *

During these years, Barb passed away suddenly, leaving Syd bereft. We were glad to be old friends he could count on for some simple company, a walk in the woods, and a cup of tea.

At one point we decided to clean out our barn, where we stored things we might want someday. I found a large cardboard box filled with all my files relating to Syd and the books. As I went through it for the first time in thirty years I found hundreds of pages of Syd's writings, just as he had given them to me for inclusion in the books. Also, letters he had sent me, other amazing memorabilia, and it occurred to me this was all very important and should be included in a kind of Sydney Banks Archives someday.

One day I gave the box to Syd, and we didn't even look over what was in the box. Years later I heard he had looked through the hundreds of pages and at one point began crying as he read the beautiful words that had come to him out of the universe so long ago; words he had forgotten he had written or even conceived of.

Sometime in the 1990s, Syd told us he would be speaking at a large gathering in Vancouver. He invited Bill and I and extended a free invitation to the talk. We were hesitant at perhaps getting involved with "the group" again, but we agreed to go. I was very curious, also.

It was a huge gathering and Syd, as always, walked up to his chair out in front, sat down and spent a few moments collecting himself. I knew he was "going inside" as he always did before his talks. He began to speak, and my heart lifted! It was the old Syd. The words came pouring forth, and it was like old times. He was "on," inspired, and the talk was just coming through him the way it always had.

After about ten minutes, he paused, as he always did, and asked if there were any questions. A young woman whom I knew well, an old student, stood up. "Syd," she said, in a very excited voice, "you've just come back from Maui! Can you tell us about your trip?"

Syd paused. I knew this was not exactly the kind of question he was after that would inspire him with answers even he had not thought of before. But, he gamely continued and spoke for a few minutes about the beach at Lahaina, how he loved it there, and how it was so easy to get into an uplifted consciousness amidst such beautiful surroundings.

The next question seemed equally off-topic and I felt Syd never again was able to return to that inspired state where he went "beyond mind," as he had called it in those early days. After a whole weekend of this, to me it never seemed to go anywhere. For me, personally, I wasn't much interested in hearing talk of the psychological.

Surprisingly, the next Monday morning Syd was at our door bright and early. Over tea, he immediately wanted to know what I had thought of the first talk I had attended in over fifteen years. I hesitated. I was almost afraid to be honest, but over the intervening years I had realized Syd and I were now friends, no longer teacher and student.

"Well," I replied, "it was not for me."

His answer was quiet and curious.

"How would you like it to have been?" he asked.

"Well," I thought, "I guess maybe — more sacred!" I thought of those hushed evenings in the Banks' home so many years before.

"More silent," I added.

Syd looked at me intently, and then spoke. I admit I was shocked by his reply.

"They don't understand the silence," he said.

Syd and I had spoken previously several times about how his teachings had changed, and I knew terms such as "Christ-consciousness," "God" and "The Spiritual Life" were no longer part of his teaching. Although I'd had twelve years of Catholic convent school and so was quite comfortable with those terms, for many these terms related to that old paradigm of "established religion" and "church," and many people, including those Syd now wanted to reach, might be turned off by them. In the interest of helping more people, when Syd had decided to eliminate these terms, I believe he was able to help tens of thousands more students to hear his message.

Years later, during another tea, another talk, Syd shared the latest news of his foray into the world of universities and colleges, teaching psychologists and therapists the new paradigm. He went on for quite a while, and I found it uninspiring compared to those heady early days when it was all so direct, so spiritual.

"I'm not interested in all that psychological stuff," I ventured. "When I needed help, I had spoken to therapists, crisis center people, psychologists, psychiatrists and none of them helped. Nothing helped until I met you. I'm on the spiritual path," I said.

Syd looked sad and quietly answered, and again I was shocked and remember his answer to this day.

"They don't understand the spiritual," he said.

EPILOGUE

When Sydney Banks appeared at my door on one of his last visits before his passing in May of 2009 and said, "I'm not going to be around forever," Syd was wrong.

Sydney Banks, the not-so-ordinary man, will live on forever in the hearts and minds of those he helped, advised, saved, rescued and inspired. In both the books we wrote together and through his other books, in scores of tapes, DVDs and interviews, Syd's wisdom *will* live on forever.

In decades and generations to come the story of his amazing transformation, from the "simple ordinary welder" who experiences a classic enlightenment to the world-renowned teacher, will continue his legacy.

"Someday," Syd continued on that visit, "someone is going to have to tell my story, and you are the only one who can do it!"

In the fullness of time, writing this book and in so doing delving back into the past and reliving the story of how I came to meet such a one, has shown me that, indeed, I was the one to tell Syd's story, for I find that in telling my own story, I have been telling his.

I trust that Syd, in his now eternal life, and reading *Encounters with an Enlightened Man* will have a good chuckle and enjoy reading these words as much as I have enjoyed writing them.

April 4, 2017

CPSIA information can be obtained
at www.ICGtesting.com
Printed in the USA
LVHW030245260122
709252LV00004B/46